IMAGES OF WAR **SPECIAL**
THE PANZER IV
HITLER'S ROCK

Smiling and confident-looking black-clad panzertruppen with their Panzer IV Ausf B in Poland in 1939.

IMAGES OF WAR **SPECIAL**
THE PANZER IV
HITLER'S ROCK

ANTHONY TUCKER-JONES

Illustrated by
David Lee Hemingway

Pen & Sword
MILITARY

First published in Great Britain in 2017 by
PEN & SWORD MILITARY
an imprint of
Pen & Sword Books Ltd,
47 Church Street,
Barnsley,
South Yorkshire.
S70 2AS

A CIP record for this book is available from the British Library.

ISBN 978 1 47385 675 2

Printed and bound by Gutenberg Press, Malta

Pen & Sword Books Ltd incorporates the Imprints of Pen & Sword Aviation, Pen & Sword Maritime, Pen & Sword Military, Wharncliffe Local History, Pen & Sword Select, Pen & Sword Military Classics and Leo Cooper.

For a complete list of Pen & Sword titles please contact
Pen & Sword Books Limited
47 Church Street, Barnsley, South Yorkshire, S70 2AS, England
E-mail: enquiries@pen-and-sword.co.uk
Website: www.pen-and-sword.co.uk

Contents

Introduction

The more powerful Panther and Tiger tanks have always eclipsed the Panzer IV and yet it played a far more pivotal role throughout the entire course of the Second World War. Likewise it outshone its stablemate the Panzer III, which was eventually abandoned as a gun tank. As well as providing a well-rounded tank, the Panzer IV also supplied a highly versatile platform for a whole family of self-propelled guns and tank destroyers.

These different types of Panzer IV saw combat with both the German Army and the Waffen-SS in all the major theatres of operation. In addition the Panzer IV was widely deployed by Hitler's Axis allies. It was supplied in limited quantities to Bulgaria, Croatia, Finland, Hungary, Italy and Romania, as well as Spain and Turkey. In some cases it was subsequently turned against the Germans.

The British Army first encountered the Panzer IV in France in 1940, where its low-velocity gun was not a great threat to the very heavily armoured but cripplingly slow Matilda II tank. Rommel lost a number of Panzer IV at Arras in the face of a valiant but ill-fated British counter-attack. However, in the deserts of North Africa the greater range of the early Panzer IV's high explosive shells gave it a distinct advantage before British tanks could close.

Once it was up-gunned it enjoyed an even greater advantage and came into its own as a gun tank. Luckily for the British the latter were never deployed in great numbers in Libya and Tunisia. In Russia and Normandy it was a different matter and the Panzer IV became the workhorse of the panzer divisions. On the Eastern Front the Panzer IV ultimately proved a worthy adversary of the highly-respected T-34 medium tank.

Although the Panzer IV went into production in the late 1930s, there were 50 per cent less than Russia's brand-new T-34 by 1941. Nor was it produced in significant quantities until late 1942. Despite going on to form the backbone of Hitler's panzer divisions, the Panzer IV actually started life as an infantry support tank and was not intended as a battle tank. Its low-velocity gun, also fitted to the Sturmgeschütz III, was designed to fire high explosive rounds and not armour piercing. Nonetheless, Hitler's early Mk IVs initially proved useful during his Blitzkrieg into the West and Russia.

While the Panzer III was a good design at the start of the war, it rapidly became clear that its 50mm anti-tank gun was inadequate against the newer Soviet tanks armed with a 76.2mm gun. This 50mm gun had a much higher velocity than the weapon on the Panzer IV. Therefore it was obvious soon after the invasion of the Soviet Union that the T-34 outmatched both the Panzer III and the Panzer IV. This inevitably led to an arms race as both sides sought to produce a more effective tank killer. In addition to up-gunning the Panzer IV, to counter the T-34 the Germans came up with the Tiger and the Panther but these were never built in decisive numbers.

While the Panzer III was completely given over to assault gun production, the up-gunned Panzer IV was kept in production as a gun tank, seeing combat in one form or another throughout the whole of the Second World War. The Panzer IV had an ardent supporter in General Heinz Guderian in his role as Inspector-General of Armoured Troops. It was he who lobbied to keep it in service even when newer types of panzer were being put into the field. Guderian never saw the over-engineered Panther and Tiger as viable solutions to the panzer divisions' problem warding off ever-growing numbers of enemy tanks.

In fact, despite Nazi engineering ingenuity, they were never able to dispense with the Mk IV's services, which became the equivalent of the Russian T-34 and American M4 Sherman. However, although it appeared in a number of successful guises, the Mk IV was never up-gunned to the extent that it became a decisive weapon in the same manner that the later T-34/85 tank did.

There were ten different production models of the Panzer IV – essentially they all looked the same, though the last four types sported a very distinctive long-barrelled anti-tank gun. It was these later models that were the real tank killers. Otherwise ongoing changes mainly related to improving the powerpack and enhancing the armour. In all some 8,500 Panzer IV were built from 1937 to 1945.

Throughout the war older models of the Panzer IV were progressively upgraded. This meant that they often had a mix-and-match of different parts, making it on occasions difficult to precisely identify photographs of retrofitted models. In addition there were three types of Panzer IV tank destroyer and a self-propelled anti-tank gun. These and other various specialized tracked armoured fighting vehicles, including self-propelled anti-aircraft guns, accounted for another 4,900 Panzer IV chassis.

As a good all-rounder the Panzer IV was a greatly respected adversary on both the Eastern and Western Fronts. It was on the battlefields of North Africa's deserts, Russia's steppe and Normandy's hedgerows that the Panzer IV gained its tough reputation for reliability and hitting power. Such was the bravery and tenacity of the crews that Panzer IVs were even known to tackle the mighty Joseph Stalin heavy tank. Ultimately the Panzer IV proved vastly more reliable and numerous than the Tiger and the Panther. In this respect it proved to be the better of the three and therefore was arguably the best panzer of the Second World War.

Photograph Sources

All photographs in this book are sourced via the author.

Chapter One

Early Days
– Ausf A-C

Development of Hitler's Panzer Mk IV medium support tank commenced in the mid-1930s at the same time as that of the Mk III medium tank. The latter was codenamed the Zugführerwagen (platoon commander's vehicle) and the former the Bataillonsführerwagen (battalion commander's vehicle), so were dubbed the ZW and BW series respectively. Each was assigned differing roles. As early as 1930 the German Army High Command, through the Heereswaffenamt Wa Prüf VI (Army Ordnance Department 6), had requested that Krupp and Rheinmetall-Borsig each produce a support tank prototype. This had to be done secretly, along with all other tank development, because of the restrictions on German rearmament following the First World War.

The first prototype was dubbed the Vollkettenkraftfahrzeug 2001, which translates as fully-tracked experimental vehicle. Built in 1935 the Rheinmetall-Borsig Rh-B BW VK2001, with four pairs of road wheels, three return rollers, front drive sprocket and rear idler, was powered by a 300PS motor giving a speed of 35km/hr. This 18-ton prototype utilized the Wilson type steering and many of the design features were later incorporated into the development of the Krupp BW.

That same year Krupp-Gruson and Maschinenfabrik & Augsburg-Nurnberg also produced competing prototypes. A Daimler design never got much further than the drawing board. Interestingly all the initial drawings for the Daimler, Krupp and MAN plans had large inter-leaved road wheels, a feature that was later incorporated in the Panther and Tiger tanks. Following trials at the Kümmersdorf and Ulm testing grounds in southern Germany, the Krupp model was selected as the most promising. The MAN prototype was too high and the Rheinmetall-Borsig pilot model had a vulnerable external suspension mechanism for the road wheels.

Ausf A

While the first Panzer III built by Daimler-Benz, armed with a 37mm gun, was initially intended to be in the 15-ton category, the Panzer IV, armed with a 75mm gun, was supposed to be five tons heavier. In reality wartime requirements meant that both tanks ended up over 20 tons with the final production models being 23 tons and 25 tons respectively. Both looked very similar and required a five-man crew, but the Panzer III ultimately proved problematic as it was very difficult to up-gun the turret.

Krupp was issued the development contract for the 7.5cm Geschütz-Panzerwagen (Vs Kfz 618) or the experimental 75mm gun armoured vehicle No.618. Rather confusingly the Panzer III was designated the 37mm gun armoured vehicle N.619. Geschütz-Panzerwagen was then altered to Panzerkampfwagen (tank armoured fighting vehicle) or PzKpfw for short in 1937. The Panzer IV was re-designated the Vs Kfz 622 which was originally assigned to the Panzer II armed with a 20mm gun.

What gave the Panzer IV a better punch from the infantry's point of view than the Mk III was its short-barrelled low-velocity 75mm KwK37 L/24 gun (KwK – Kampfwagenkanone or tank gun). This was primarily a close-support weapon designed mainly for firing high explosive shells. Therefore ammunition comprised 65 per cent HE, 25 per cent armour-piercing and 10 per cent smoke rounds. Its armour-piercing capability was relatively poor due to the low muzzle velocity. Nonetheless, it had a much greater range. As a result the Panzer III was later up-gunned with a more effective 50mm weapon.

The 37mm KwK L/46.5 on the first five models of Panzer III depended on ammunition having a muzzle velocity of 745m/s and at 100m could penetrate 34mm of armour or at 500m some 29mm. The 75mm L/24 could manage less than 400m/s. It was electrically fired with a semi-automatic breech action. The inner main gun mantlet on the Panzer IV featured a right-hand coaxial MG34 machine gun (fitted on the A, B and C models), with a second one in a ball mount on the right-hand side of the superstructure on the Ausf A. The KwK37 was also used on the early model Sturmgeschütz III which had the same role as the initial Panzer IV.

The Panzer IV consisted of four major sub-assemblies – the hull, front and rear superstructure and the turret. These were all bolted together in the final assembly stage. The hull itself was divided into three by two bulkheads. The engine was positioned in the rear with the drive shaft powering the front sprockets running forward to the driving compartment under the fighting compartment floor. The gearbox was located in the middle of the front compartment, with the driver to the left and the radio operator to the right. The superstructure overhung the hull sides, allowing good internal storage.

Visibility was provided for the tank commander by a prominent vertical drum cupola with a total of eight vision slits. This was the same type as that used on the Panzer III Ausf B and had a similar overhang on the rear turret plate. The turret's power traverse was driven by a 500cc two-stroke petrol engine located to the left of the main engine. A number of pistol ports and vision slits were installed throughout the turret and hull.

Whereas the driver and hull gunner's front plate was flat on the Panzer III, on the early IVs the driver's section was stepped forward of the rest of the superstructure. This feature permitted the driver to see to his right as well as giving more ammunition storage space. The driver also had a forward-facing vision port and binocular episcope. Roof hatches served both the driver and radio operator. Hinged flaps on the glacis plate gave access to the steering mechanism and gearbox.

The initial Panzer IV was powered by a V-12 cylinder 230hp Maybach engine (first the HL 108TR and then the HL 120TRM – also used in the Panzer III), which gave a speed of 31km/hr and a range of 150km. Subsequent improvements to the engine would provide later models a speed of 40km/hr and a range of 200km. The drive was powered by the gasoline engine via a five speed transmission with an epicyclic clutch and brake steering system.

Each side of the hull had four pairs of rubber-tyred road wheels with a front drive sprocket and adjustable rear idler, plus four upper return rollers. This immediately made the Panzer IV easy to distinguish from the Panzer III, which only had three pairs of road wheels and three return rollers. On the Panzer IV the rear roller was set slightly lower than the others in order to run the track down onto the idler which was set lower than the sprocket.

The suspension was of leaf spring design rather than the much newer torsion bar system. This was in part as a result of Krupp-Gruson drawing on its experience with the Panzer I. The mounting bracket for the bogies and suspension was bolted to the side and base of the hull. Under the leading axle of each bogie were quarter-elliptic leaf springs, with the tail of the spring resting under a trailing axle on a roller.

Up to the Ausf E the Panzer IV idler wheel was fabricated from steel plate. The metal tracks were the single pin skeleton type utilising a central triple guide horn to slot the links together. This meant they could be manufactured lighter than other tracks and were suitable for almost all terrain types. The first tracks consisted of 101 links either side, were 38cm wide and cast from manganese steel. From the Ausf F onwards the tracks were widened by a modest 2cm.

Production of the Panzer IV Ausf (Model) A commenced in the autumn of 1937, with a total of just thirty-five completed by Krupp-Gruson by March 1938. This small number rather suggested that it was just another developmental prototype undergoing extensive trials. However, all of them were accepted for service by the army with the first three being issued to the panzertruppen in January 1938. The numbers actually reflected their support role and there was a greater requirement for the Panzer III. By April that year thirty were in service and the Ausf A went on to see combat in Poland, Norway and France.

The main drawback with the Ausf A was that its very thin armour – just 15mm – was no better than the initial Panzer III's and it was slower than the latter. Access for the driver and radio operator was not ideal as they both had two-piece hatches that opened backward and forward. The rear section could catch on the main gun barrel and the mantlet. As a result it was withdrawn before the spring campaigns of 1941.

Ausf B

The frontal armour on the next three models, Ausf B–D, was doubled to 30mm. Krupp-Gruson were instructed to produce forty-five improved Ausf B in April 1938 but only forty-two were finished due to problems with parts. Key changes from the A model included the doubling of the frontal armour and a more powerful 300hp Maybach HL120 TR engine and a six-speed SSG 76 transmission. This boosted the speed from 31km/hr to 40km/hr.

The Ausf B also had a new type of stepped cupola, offering better protection for the commander. Other differences involved the installation of single-piece hatches over the driver and radio operator that only opened forward. The superstructure front was also one straight piece, thereby losing the A model's step, with the hull MG 34 replaced by a visor and pistol port. Limited numbers of Ausf B saw combat in Poland, France, the Balkans and Russia. They were phased out through attrition by late 1943.

Ausf C

Just as the limited production run of the Ausf B was coming to an end, work started on the 3rd series BW or Ausf C. This proved to be the most numerous of the first three models with 134 built between September 1938 and August 1939. The Inspectorate for Engineers was also provided with six chassis for bridge-laying tanks. The initial Ausf C order had been for 300 tanks, but this was cut by 160 before production even started.

Changes on the Ausf C were largely internal with an improved turret race (or fitting), engine mount, redesigned gun mantlet housing and armoured sleeve to protect the coaxial machine gun. The engine was uprated to the Maybach HL 120TRM. Like its predecessor the Ausf C was progressively up-armoured with bolt on armoured plates and remained in service until 1943.

A few of the early model Panzer IVs continued in service well into 1944, which were not upgraded. For example, the 21st Panzer Division had half a dozen Ausf B or C still with the short 75mm gun and the 116th Panzer Division had three on its books. They should have been brought up to G and H standard by this stage of the war. These outdated models were presumably employed for training or as observations tanks (in the case of one its crew were photographed shopping for cheese!). Nonetheless, they ended up being sent into action in France.

At the end of August 1944 one of the Ausf B/C belonging to 21st Panzer was photographed abandoned in Normandy that had clearly not been up-gunned or up-armoured. It was still armed with the 24-calibre 75mm gun, had a pistol port instead of a hull machine gun and featured the narrow 36cm tracks. It looked undamaged and one of the glacis access hatches was missing, indicating it had broken down rather than been knocked out.

The Panzer IV Ausf A is immediately identifiable by its distinctive drum cupola and forward driver's position. All Panzer IV had eight road wheels and four return rollers (except for the final Ausf J, some of which only had three return rollers). Krupp-Gruson built just thirty-five of the A model from October 1937 to March 1938.

This Ausf A was photographed during the invasion of Poland in 1939. The solid white cross or balkenkruez was specific to this particular campaign. The design was soon abandoned as it made the tank far too conspicuous. The white tactical number painted over the turret vision port indicates it is the third tank of the third troop in the fourth company.

The crew have removed the right-hand drive sprocket and tracks on this Ausf A. Limited numbers of the Ausf A saw combat not only in Poland but also Norway and France before being withdrawn from the panzer regiments prior the spring campaigns of 1941.

Ausf B or C being given a warm welcome in Poland in 1939.

The burnt and smashed remains of a Panzer IV – the armoured sleeve protecting the coaxial machine gun identifies it as a C model. It has lost its glacis plate after taking a direct hit.

The Ausf C was almost identical to the Ausf B, having minor modifications to its armour and internal fittings.

Note the drive sprocket on this early Panzer IV: from the Ausf E it was a much more simplified design. This tank bears the emblem of the 11th Panzer Division.

The drive assembly to the front sprocket has been removed from this Ausf C, showing the gearing from the brake/steering unit. Also clearly visible is the new type of turret cupola fitted to the Ausf B and C that replaced the early drum cupola on the Ausf A.

Chapter Two

Ramping up Production – Ausf D-F

Improvements to the Panzer IV were largely driven by the regular need to enhance the armour. The problem with this was that the Panzerwaffe were issued with a constantly-changing tank, which was a mixed blessing as they did not have the same capabilities – the Panzerwaffe faced exactly the same problem with the similarly-evolving Panzer III.

Ausf D

Confusingly the Ausf D was known as the 4th and 5th series Panzer IV. Krupp was instructed to build 200 in the 4th Series BW and 48 in the 5th Series BW in January 1938. In the event just 229 were finished as gun tanks, the remaining nineteen chassis being used for sixteen bridge-laying tanks, two self-propelled gun mounts and an ammunition carrier for the super-heavy Karl mortar. Also, as part of the experiments to up-gun the Panzer IV, an Ausf D was fitted with a 50mm KwK39 L/60, which had double the muzzle velocity of the 75mm KwK37 L/24 and therefore vastly better penetration.

The Ausf D had its side and rear armour enhanced from the 15mm of its predecessors to 20mm, and the main gun was fitted with an external mantlet. The front of the superstructure was once more stepped with the driver forward of the radio operator. The driver was provided with a pistol port to his right and the hull machine gun was reinstated for the radio operator. Ausf Ds at the tail-end of the production run had 30mm plates bolted and welded to the hull front and superstructure front as well as an extra 20mm on the sides in 1943. A few Ausf D were armed with the long-barrelled 75mm KwK L/48 gun and deployed with training and replacement units. This gun was installed in late Ausf G and the subsequent H and J models.

Production of the Panzer IV support tank was such that by May 1940 every tank unit with a medium tank company could deploy six to eleven Mk IVs. At the start of the invasion of France on 10 May 1940 Hitler's panzer divisions were able to field a total of 280 Ausf A, B, C and D. Before it was phased out in 1944 the Ausf D saw action in France, the Balkans, Africa and Russia.

Ausf E

The 6th Series Ausf E went into production in September 1940. It had a new design of cupola, other modifications to the turret and increased armour. The turret rear now had a single bent plate, which eliminated the cupola overhang. In addition the turret roof was fitted with an exhaust fan to remove noxious gun fumes from the fighting compartment. The front of the Ausf E hull had 50mm of armour, with 20mm plate bolted on the hull and superstructure sides. Other modifications included countersinking the glacis hatches level with the surface of the glacis, a new driver's visor that pivoted and a simplified drive sprocket. In total forty Ausf D and E were shipped to North Africa while some 438 Ausf B to F were committed to the assault on the Soviet Union. Like its predecessor, the Ausf E was phased out in 1944.

Ausf F

Whereas the Ausf A, B, C, D and E Panzer IV had all been produced by Krupp-Gruson, construction of the Ausf F, or Ausf F1 as it became known, was extended to the manufacturers Nibelungenwerke and Vomag. Krupp was initially instructed to build 500 of the Panzer IV 7th series, but Vomag then received an order for 100 and Nibelungenwerke for 25. However, the German Army wanted the Panzer IV up-gunned with the long-barrel 75mm KwK40 L/43 anti-tank gun as soon as possible to produce the F2. The result was that twenty-five of the F1 were converted before they were ever issued to the panzertruppen.

Once again the main improvement on the Ausf F1 was an increase in armour, which meant that it was a ton heavier than the Ausf E. The change in the armour also required modifications to the driver's visor (with installation of the Fahrersehklappe 50), vision ports, pistol ports, turret doors and the hull machine-gun fitting (the Kugelblende 50 ball mount replacing the Kugelblende 30 gimbal mount). The turret side door in previous models comprised a single hatch either side, but on the F double doors replaced these to make access easier. The glacis hatches also featured raised air intake cowls to cool the steering brakes.

From the Ausf F1 onward the rear idler wheel was simplified and fabricated from tubular steel with plate reinforcing webs. This had seven rather than the previous eight spokes. Likewise the tracks were modified on the F1 with a reduction of links from 101 to 99. Also the track width increased from 38cm to 40cm to help spread the ground pressure of the tank.

The F1 was mainly used as combat replacements, but several new units were equipped with it and it refitted the 2nd and 5th Panzer Divisions. Some 208 Ausf B–F1 were in the field when Hitler commenced Operation Blue his summer offensive on the Eastern Front in June 1942. By the time of the Kursk offensive the following summer these had been reduced to just sixty tanks.

The 4th and 5th Series Panzer IV was known as the Ausf D. Like the initial Ausf A, it also had the driver's position set forward of the radio operator's position, creating a step in the superstructure front plate. However, it had an external mantlet for the main gun.

The crew of this Ausf D are making sure they do not run out of fuel while on operations. The turret has been stacked with 'Jerricans'. The panzers also used towed trailers during operational deployment.

This D model was photographed while on exercise in early 1940. Like the earlier versions the cupola overhung the rear of the turret. An equipment bustle or storage bin was normally attached to the rear of the Panzer IV turret.

This Ausf D lost its turret and part of the engine during the fighting in France. Note the pistol port to the right-hand side of the driver's visor. A direct hit or the ammunition 'cooking off' caused the damage.

Another knocked-out Ausf D.

Amongst an assortment of Panzer IIIs and IIs, this Panzer IV Ausf D was a casualty of the fighting in Libya. The crew attempted to increase the armour by adding track links to the front and the driver's compartment and the turret. The road wheel on the turret was also intended to serve the same purpose.

The drive sprocket on the Ausf E was simplified, making it easier to manufacturer and stronger. Likewise, it had a different cupola to the Ausf B and C.

Improvements on the Ausf E included installing an extractor fan in the turret to remove gun fumes. The circular vent can be seen on the right side of the turret roof. In addition the glacis hatches were countersunk level with the glacis surface and it had a pivoting driver's visor.

Panzertruppen examine a badly-damaged Ausf D in Libya. This model, along with the E and F1, were the most common in North Africa, making up 25 per cent of Rommel's armoured formations. It had the distinct advantage of being able to fire both high explosive and armour piercing rounds – British tanks could only fire armour piercing at close range.

Whitewashed for winter operations, these Auf E are being shipped to Russia. The large barrel-shaped object at the back of the tank is the engine silencer and exhaust outlet – the design of this changed as development of the Panzer IV progressed.

The Ausf F1 went into production in April 1941. New features included raised air-intake cowls on the glacis hatches. The front of the superstructure had a single 50mm plate with a new machine-gun ball mount and an improved visor for the driver.

The sprocket was now dish-shaped on the Ausf FI and the idler had seven tubular steel spokes rather than the previous design with eight made from steel plate. The turret doors were also replaced by double hatches either side.

The Kugelblende 50 ball mount for the hull machine gun on this FI had been covered to prevent fouling by the mud.

To combat the dust being thrown up in Russia this F1 crew are wearing goggles.

This F1 has some sort of large storage box attached to the glacis plate.

Chapter Three

Something 'Special' – Ausf F2

By late 1941 it was very apparent that the 76.2mm gun mounted in the Soviet KV-1 heavy and T-34 medium tanks was superior to that of the Panzer IV's short 75mm gun. This meant it was imperative to install the much more powerful long-barrelled 75mm KwK40 L/43 anti-tank gun as quickly as possible. This process had started in the winter of 1941 and the intention was that this would commence with the Ausf G in May 1942. However, to speed things up it was decided to co-opt Ausf F production first.

Ausf F2

A month's worth of production of the Ausf F was disrupted in March 1942 in order to create the F2. The introduction of this model saw the length of the 75mm gun increased from 24 to 43 calibres. To compensate for the long barrel a coil-spring counter-balance was installed. It was designed to act as both an anti-tank and a high explosive firing weapon. None of its parts were interchangeable with the earlier gun, but like the 75mm KwK37 L/24 it was electrically fired and had a semi-automatic breech action. The barrel was fitted with a muzzle brake of which there were about four different types.

Initially the KwK40 L/43 was fitted with a very distinctive globular single-baffle muzzle brake, which was followed by a series of double baffle designs. As there was a two or three-month overlap in production of both the F2 and the subsequent Ausf G, which came out of the same Krupp, Nibelungenwerke and Vomag factories, there was inevitably some overlap in appearance and design modifications. Essentially they were the same tank, with the F2 being the interim version.

In the summer of 1942 the Ausf G went over to the double-baffle muzzle brake and it is quite possible some of the later F2 featured this. Similarly some up-gunned Panzer IVs sent to the Eastern Front, while they had the single baffle muzzle brake, also had the newer-style Ausf G turret that eliminated the side vision ports.

The L/43 was a fundamental upgrade because it changed the Panzer IV's primary role from being a support weapon to a tank-to-tank weapon. It also meant it firmly superseded the Panzer III on the battlefield. From the F2 onwards the Panzer IV went from being a medium support tank to a medium battle tank. The StuG III assault gun went through exactly the same evolution when its close support weapon was upgraded to create the StuG Ausf F.

The earlier L/24 gun had a muzzle velocity of 385m/s and could penetrate 41mm of armour at 100m, 39mm at 400mm and 35mm at 1,000m. This degraded to 33mm and 30mm at 1,500m and 2,000m respectively but at such ranges accuracy was a problem. In contrast the much more powerful long-barrel L/43 had a muzzle velocity of 740m/s and could cut through almost 100mm of armour at 100m, 90mm at 500m and 80mm at 1,000m.

This was exactly what the Panzerwaffe needed at this crucial moment in the war. It was only now that the Panzer IV truly came into its own and was to remain the backbone of the Panzerwaffe for the rest of the war despite the appearance of the Tiger and Panther. From mid-1942 onwards the Panzer IV began to take over the role of the Panzer III. Shortly after the chassis of the latter was given over to assault gun production.

Provision for full indirect fire was never made on German tanks. On the Panzer IV targeting of the main gun was achieved using a fixed-eyepiece telescope-type sight, known as the TZF5b manufactured by E. Leitz of Wetzlar. This had compound object glass and moving graticules giving magnification of about 2.5 times for the main gun and the coaxial machine gun. In the Ausf F2 and G a clinometer was fitted to measure the angle of elevation.

The main differences between the F1 and F2 other than the barrel length, involved ammunition storage design which had to be modified to allow for the larger rounds. The commander and gunner's seats were altered to allow more ammunition to be carried. An auxiliary hand traverse was fitted for use by the loader and the elevation mechanism was modified. The commander's cupola was also moved slightly forward.

When the F2 pitched up in North Africa the British dubbed it the 'Mk IV Special' with good reason. The heaviest British anti-tank gun could not compete. The 75mm gun on the American-supplied M3 Grant tank was inferior to the F2's because it could only penetrate 45mm of armour at 1,000 yards.

German designers looked at ways of up-gunning the Ausf F even further. An experimental mock up was produced of a Panzer IV F2 armed with a 75mm KwK 42 L/70. Although this weapon did not feature a muzzle brake the barrel length made the tank very nose-heavy and unwieldy. The L/70 was at least twice as long as the L/43 and on the Ausf F was not really a practical design for a gun tank. While this up-gunned variant of the F2 did not go into production, the gun with muzzle brake was later employed on the Panther, which appeared in 1943. Similarly it was used the following summer to arm the Panzer IV/70 tank destroyer but without a muzzle brake. This Panzer IV variant again proved nose-heavy, which resulted in excessive wear on the front road wheels.[*]

The Ausf F was similarly used as an experimental mount for a weapon using the Gerlich principle. The Panzer IV F with Waffe 0725 featured a gun using a tapered-bore barrel of 75/55mm. This fired a skirted round that was compressed as it travelled along the bore of the barrel, which greatly increased the velocity of the projectile. The round had added punch thanks to a core of tungsten-carbide, but a shortage of the latter meant that the project was not viable and this F2 variant was also abandoned. Instead it was decided the best way to improve the armament of the Ausf F was to install the larger-calibre KwK40 L/48, which led to the Ausf G.

Between March and July 1942 some 200 interim Ausf F2 were produced including the 25 converted from F1. By the summer of 1942 there were 135 Panzer IVs with the L/43 gun on the Eastern Front. This could penetrate the T-34 out to a range of 1,600m. Although the Tiger, armed with an 88mm gun, appeared late that year it was not available in any great numbers, leaving the Panzer IV to do all the work. The Panther armed with a 75mm gun that was more powerful than the Ausf F2/G/H did not appear until the summer of 1943.

---

[*] For further information on the Panzer IV/70 see the author's *German Assault Guns and Tank Destroyers 1940-1945* also published by Pen & Sword.

With the advent of the Ausf F2 the Panzer IV became a true gun tank. German officers examine a new F2 which is easily recognizable by the early single-baffle globular muzzle brake fitted to the Kwk40 L/43 75mm gun. Later models were equipped with at least four different types of larger double-baffle muzzle brake.

The F2 began to arrive in North Africa in the summer of 1942 where the British dubbed it the Panzer IV 'Special'. It posed a threat to the under-gunned and under-armoured tanks of the 8th Army but was never available in sufficient numbers to tilt the balance.

The cupola on this tank has been blasted off. Rommel received just twenty-seven F2s by August 1942. The Panzer III remained the main German tank type in North Africa.

Deployment of the F2 on the Eastern Front provided much-needed parity with the ever-growing number of T-34s.

This F2 was photographed while on garrison duty in occupied France.

Panzer IV with the KwK40 early muzzle brake lost on the Eastern Front – interestingly it has no vision ports forward of the doors on the sides of the turret, suggesting that this is an early Ausf G or late-production F2.

This could be a late-production F2 with the new muzzle brake fighting in Tunisia. The lack of visible turret vision ports forward of the side hatch indicated it is an Ausf G which was quite rare in North Africa.

This Panzer IV was photographed on 10 May 1943 in Tunisia shortly before the German surrender. Judging by the muzzle brake and the lack of turret vision ports this is an early Ausf G.

The more numerous Ausf G first appeared on the Eastern Front during the summer of 1942, shortly after the F2.

Chapter Four

Panzerwaffe Backbone
– Ausf G–H

The next two production models, the Ausf G and H also armed with the KwK40, formed the bulk of the Mk IV panzer force, with 1,687 Gs and 3,774 Hs built during 1942 to 1944. From 1943 panzer divisions were meant to have one battalion equipped with Mk IVs and one with Panthers, but due to problems with the latter this often did not happen. The net result was that there were always more Panzer IVs than Panthers. Most of the Ausf G went to Russia while in 1944 most of the Mk IVs in France were Ausf H supplemented by Ausf J.

Ausf G

The Panzer IV Ausf G first went into production in May 1942 and was initially armed with the same main gun as the interim F2. Visually there was very little to distinguish the two. Notably, on the G model the vision ports on the sides of the turret were dispensed with as well as the one serving the loader's position on the front of the turret. By the summer of 1942 other alterations included a new muzzle brake and a system that permitted siphoning coolant from one panzer to another to help cold-weather starting. The smoke dispensers were also moved from the rear of the hull to the turret sides.

It was very quickly decided to up-armour some of the G model. From 20 June 1942 deliveries included additional 30mm armour plate bolted or welded to the front of the hull and superstructure. This gave the tank a total of 80mm on the front. It had been hoped to boost it to 100mm, but trials showed the Ausf G became too nose heavy and difficult to steer. From July to November 1942 every month some sixteen production tanks were fitted with the additional protection. From December 1942 the number went up to 50 per cent of all production tanks which resulted in about 700 Ausf G having the extra armour.

At the beginning of 1943 the driver's KFF2 episcope on the Ausf G was removed. Also that year spaced armour consisting of thin steel plates or panels hung from steel brackets, known as Schürzen or skirts, were added to the sides of the hull and the sides and rear of the turret in response to a fresh Soviet threat. Hence the removal of the turret's side vision ports. To allow the turret side access doors to open hinged double doors were fitted to either side of the 8mm turret skirts. Despite these it was possible to escape via the turret without using the doors in the spaced plates.

The 5mm hull Schürzen consisted of six plates either side with the front two and the rear one tapered. The foremost was the smallest and created a greater taper than at the back, but this was easily damaged and often absent. These skirts covered the hull and superstructure, the return rollers and a quarter of the drive sprocket and idler. The eight road wheels were left exposed.

Made of mild steel boiler plate, the Schürzen were intended to help defend the tank against attack from the new Soviet RPG-43 shaped-charge high explosive anti-tank (HEAT) hand grenade and later hollow-charge weapons such as the American Bazooka and the British PIAT (Portable Infantry Anti-Tank). The RPG-43 entered service in 1943 and could penetrated 75mm of armour at a 90° angle. Although it had to be thrown at very close range, it gave no warning like other anti-tank weapons. The skirts would prematurely detonate an incoming projectile inches in front of the main armour and dissipate the force of the HEAT round. Although the plate would be destroyed, it saved the tank from direct impact. The hull Schürzen were fragile and easily damaged in combat or torn off whilst the tank was on the move. As a result the additional turret skirts tended to last a lot longer. Panzer IV were regularly photographed with the hull Schürzen in varying states of disrepair with sections of plate missing.

Another form of protection was added from early 1943. This was a light grey paste known as Zimmerit, which was applied to the vertical surfaces of the hulls and turrets of most tanks and assault guns. Panzer IVs were coated in the factory before painting and the paste was raked with a spreader, creating ridged and criss-cross patterns to increase the depth. The paste was then hardened off and spray-painted. This prevented the attaching of magnetic anti-tank hollow charges. On occasion the Schürzen were also coated in it. The Zimmerit patterns varied from factory to factory.

Final production Ausf G were fitted with a new type of drive sprocket and the radio antenna was moved from the right of the hull rear to the left. The later alteration made it impossible to distinguish late Ausf G from early Ausf H. The new design sprocket wheel was intended to improve traction with the tracks. Mid-model Ausf G were fitted with a double-baffle muzzle brake on the main gun used on the subsequent H and J models.

A total of 1,275 Ausf G were armed with the KwK40 L/43 gun. Then from late March 1943 the Ausf G followed by the H and J were armed with a gun with an even longer barrel, the 75mm KwK40 L/48. Although this fired the same ammunition as the 43-calibre gun, it had a barrel five calibres longer. The breech mechanism was also simplified to help with production. Nonetheless, apart from a few components, the barrel and breech rings of the 43- and 48-calibre guns were interchangeable.

Production of the Ausf G ended in June 1943. In total ten separate orders with Krupp-Gruson, Nibelungenwerke and Vomag amounted to 1,750, but only 1,687 were built as Ausf G. The rest were employed as prototypes for the Hummel (Bumble Bee) and Brummbär (Grizzly Bear) consisting of ten and fifty-three chassis respectively. When Hitler's summer offensive commenced on the Eastern Front in June 1942 he had about 170 F2 and G available. By the start of the Kursk offensive the following summer Army Groups Centre and South had 841 long-barrel Panzer IVs.

Ausf H

In early 1943 General Heinz Guderian was appointed Inspector-General of Armoured Troops. He was not impressed with the new Panzer V dubbed the Panther, which was having unending 'teething' problems. He recalled, 'In the tank production field it was decided during April, in accordance with my suggestion, that the Panzer IV should continue to be built until such time as a high level of mass-production was absolutely assured for the Panther.' Later in the year Guderian was very displeased to learn that Panzer IV production was to be partially diverted to the construction of assault guns and tank destroyers.

The Ausf H went into production in April 1943 and was by far the most numerous type of Panzer IV ever built. Once more changes from its predecessor were fairly minimal and were alterations one would expect. On the front of the H model the armour evolved from the 50mm basic plus additional 30mm to 80mm basic – inevitably this meant a sizeable weight increase by one and a half tons bringing the tank's overall weight to 25 tons. It also meant that the tank's armour had increased fourfold over that of the original version – the Ausf A.

The turret featured a better-armoured cupola, a single-piece cupola hatch hinged to the left (all the previous models had a two-piece hatch that opened in opposite directions) and a cupola mount for an anti-aircraft machine gun. On the hull, other changes involved deletion of the driver and radio operator's side vision ports to give the armour better integrity, new-style drive sprockets and idler wheels, all-steel return rollers and external air filters.

In order to give the Panzer IV better ground clearance, in 1943 designers and engineers tried to alter the suspension, which had remained largely unchanged since 1937. These experiments were not fruitful and the Panzer IV retained the same basic suspension until the end of the war.

A total of 3,935 Ausf H chassis were built, of which 3,744 were gun tanks, while 130 were diverted to Brummbär construction by Deutsche Eisenwerke. Nibelungenwerke diverted another thirty to Krupp for the initial Sturmgeschütz IV production.[*] By June 1944 some two-thirds of the Panzer IV deployed in France were the H model, the rest being the new Ausf J.

As the war progressed most of the older models of Panzer IV were recalled for upgrading. For example, the Tank Museum at Bovington has an Ausf D that was factory-modified to Ausf H specifications. This principally included installing the long-barrel KwK40 L/43 gun, while in addition the driver and hull machine gunner's positions were up-armoured using bolt on armour plate. The bow plate armour was increased and extra armour was bolted to the front plate. The turret was fitted with spaced armour and wider tracks were fitted. From a distance it looked like any other late-model Panzer IV but up close the forward driver's compartment of the Ausf D is clearly visible.

---

[*] See *German Assault Guns and Tank Destroyers 1940–1945*.

This seems to be an Ausf G fitted with the new muzzle brake, which went into production from May 1942. The Schürzen spaced armour on the turret was introduced in early 1943 along with spaced side skirts in response to a new type of Soviet anti-tank grenade.

A disabled Ausf H captured during the British advance on Villa Grande, Italy in 1943. Note the new design of single-piece hatch on the cupola. The engine silencer around the exhaust has been badly damaged. The tank has also thrown its left-hand track.

This abandoned late-production Ausf G or early Ausf H '725' was found hiding in a haystack near Szee, Italy. Modifications during the H production run included deleting the side vision ports for the driver and radio operator – this vehicle still has them fitted.

The crew of this Ausf H are repairing the tracks during the fighting at Monte Cassino in early 1944. They have left the doors open on the turret Schürzen to enable them to jump back in quickly if they come under fire.

Ausf H '802' serving with the 2nd Panzer Division was destroyed at Pontfarcy in Normandy. It has no Zimmerit and although the rail is fitted, the hull Schürzen is absent. At the beginning of June 1944 the division had ninety-four Panzer IVs.

Belonging to the 21st Panzer Division, this Ausf H was knocked out on the plain north-east of Caen near Lebisey in June 1944. This tank was fighting 'hull-down' desert-style and appears to have been further concealed by the surrounding boards. Good shooting penetrated the turret's 50mm armour. Zimmerit can be seen on the front of the superstructure and the turret.

Remains of a burnt-out Panzer IV along with other vehicles caught in the open by Allied fighter-bombers in Normandy.

This derelict Ausf H, most likely from the 13th Panzer Division, was lost during the siege of Budapest in early 1945. The gun lacks a muzzle brake.

Two Ausf H burning on the Eastern Front: the second one is just visible through the smoke on the far right. Smoke from the nearest is pouring from the side of the turret, indicating a fighting compartment fire.

Chapter Five

No Frills
– Ausf J

Guderian knew that the German armed forces could not dispense with the Panzer IV. Upon taking up his post as Inspector-General of Armoured Troops he had assessed that 'the production of the Panzer IV must be <u>increased</u> during the year 1944–45, so far as this can be done without damaging the production of Panthers and Tigers.'

The last model of the Mk IV had many features dropped during production in order to simplify and speed up construction. Notably one of the four return rollers was dispensed with as well as the pistol ports; some of the vision ports and the electric turret traverse plus the exhaust system were simplified. In the name of further expediency wire mesh screens were mounted on the sides of the hull instead of the normal Schürzen. It also had steel-tyred road wheels due to the shortage of rubber. Some 1,758 of this type were built from June 1944 to March 1945. The Ausf J saw combat in the battles for France, the Ardennes, the Rhineland and on the Eastern Front.

Ausf J

In light of problems refuelling and re-equipping in the field, German tank designers in their infinite wisdom decided to increase the Panzer IV's range by 110km. For Operation Barbarossa, tanks, including the Panzer IV, had been furnished with a field-manufactured fuel trailer. This could carry two extra 200-litre petrol tanks. The 20-litre 'Jerricans' (or jerrycan) were also strapped to the turret. However, both measures were largely temporary fixes, especially as the trailers were easily damaged.

The designers boosted the 210km range of the Ausf G and H to 320km. This was achieved by increasing the 470-litre fuel capacity of the Ausf H to 680 litres. This came at a price because the extra space needed meant removing the auxiliary engine that powered the electric turret traverse on the Ausf J. On previous models this was positioned at the rear of the hull to the left of the large exhaust outlet. A dual gear-ratio hand traverse was installed instead. This was clearly a retrograde step and slowed firing response times. On late Ausf J the bulky engine silencer and exhaust outlet was replaced by two simple vertical exhaust mufflers.

There had been some hope of installing the Panther tank turret armed with the KwK42 L/70 gun on the Panzer IV chassis. The turret proved much too heavy and overloaded the chassis and transmission. Instead, the thickness of the turret roof armour on the Ausf J was increased and for close defence a Nähverteidigungswaffe smoke projector was fitted. This final model also used at least two different types of the modified East Tracks, which gave a better overall performance. As the name suggests these were developed as a result of battlefield experience on the Eastern Front.

In North Africa the Sherman had been able to hold its own against the early-model Panzer IVs, but in Normandy the frontal 80mm hull and superstructure armour of the Ausf H and J easily resisted its 75mm gun. Only the turret remained vulnerable. Limited numbers of Shermans were up-gunned with 17-pounder or 76mm guns but these were not up-armoured, leaving them at a real disadvantage.

The first Ausf J deployed to Normandy were fitted with standard Schürzen and coated in Zimmerit. While the hull Schürzen on the Ausf G and initial Ausf J consisted of six adjoining steel plates, on later production Ausf J they were replaced by simple wire mesh. These screens consisted of only three sections but covered the same area. Also by this stage the use of Zimmerit had been discontinued and it was not applied to the final batches of Ausf J. Both types of Schürzen were fitted to the Panzer IV/70 tank destroyer – photographic evidence shows a Panzer IV/70(A) with wire-mesh skirts.

By late 1943 production of the Panzer IV was increasingly under pressure. Although Guderian supported the factories being switched solely to the Panther, retooling would simply have been too disruptive. Panther manufacture was lagging behind and by this stage Germany was increasingly on the defensive on the Eastern Front. The result of this was that the Panzer IV was kept in production and was increasingly diverted to making assault guns and tank destroyers. This was exactly the same fate that had befallen the Panzer III.

In December 1943 Krupp-Gruson finally stopped building the Panzer IV gun tank and in the New Year switched production over to the StuG IV. Likewise in January 1944 Vomag began producing the Jagdpanzer IV alongside its Panzer IV. This continued until May when tank production was abandoned in favour of the Jagdpanzer IV and then the Panzer IV/70. In August 1944 Nibelungenwerke started building its own version of the Panzer IV/70. The result of this was that Nibelungenwerke was the only company to produce the Ausf J. As well as the 1,758 gun tanks, some 278 Ausf J chassis were diverted to Panzer IV/70 production from August 1944. Another 142 chassis were converted to Brummbärs.

Production was concentrated with Nibelungenwerke for a reason – the Allied bombing offensive. The original Panzer IV prototypes had been built by Krupp-Gruson at Magdeburg. Upon series production the Krupp factories in Essen and Eisen un Huettenwerke had built the hulls and turrets. Subcomponents had come from other companies. It was only with the Ausf F/G that production needed to be shared. At this point Vomag and Nibelungenwerke became involved. In the face of escalating Allied bombing of Germany's industrial centres, the main production was then relocated to Nibelungenwerke which was out of range of the bombers.

Panzer IV Ausf H on manoeuvres in France in 1944. They have a new type of drive sprocket and idler wheel. Also the turret is fitted with the new cupola with thicker armour and a single-piece cupola hatch. The haphazard three-tone camouflage has been sprayed on with little precision.

An Ausf J with the 2nd SS Panzer Division in France: half the nearside Schürzen is missing. This was added to afford some protection from the Soviet RPG-43 anti-tank grenade.

This late-production Ausf H lacks Zimmerit – this stopped being applied in September 1944 because it was time-consuming and due to unfounded fears it might be flammable. The tank has a very crudely painted three-tone camouflage scheme.

The Schürzen are intact on this Ausf J serving in Poland in 1944. The small front plate has a distinctive notch above the sprocket, designed to prevent snagging on the tracks.

Remains of an Ausf J from the 26th Panzer Division, which fought in Italy in the Salerno and Cassino areas from January to May 1944. The hull has been shattered and the muzzle brake is clogged with dirt.

Two Ausf J belonging to the 2nd SS Panzer Division at St Fromond in Normandy in July 1944. Although the nearest tank has the standard engine muffler, the auxiliary engine for the electric-powered turret traverse is clearly missing.

Photographed near Liège in Belgium, this Ausf J with its turret reversed has a simplified twin exhaust muffler. There is evidence of Zimmerit on the rear of the hull and the front of the turret, showing it was built before September 1944.

This burnt-out Ausf J pictured in January 1945 still has the remains of its mesh-screen Schürzen. This was from the early production run as it has four return rollers: on the later Js one roller was dropped.

Colour Plates

At the start of the Second World War German military vehicles were painted in a two-tone scheme using dark grey (dunkel grau) and dark brown (dunkel braun). Irregular patches of the brown were added to break up the factory grey base coat. In mid-1940 the brown was discontinued. In Europe after the Polish campaign most panzers were grey with a white Balkenkreuz (Balkan Cross) with a black centre. Vehicles shipped to North Africa were painted dark yellow or salmon sand, over which was sometimes added a vague hint of camouflage using darker colours.

German Army Memorandum No.181, issued in February 1943, decreed that the basic overall colour for all military vehicles be a deep sand-yellow (dunkel gelb). From this point all vehicles were sprayed this colour, which superseded the previous panzer grey, before leaving the factory. This led to an enormous range of camouflage patterns being employed on the Eastern and Western Fronts as well as in Italy, using two other colours, olive green (oliv grun) and a red-brown (rotbraun) either together or singularly. During the winter on the Eastern and Western Fronts Panzer IVs were snow-camouflaged with varying degrees of success using a whitewash finish.

Panzer IVs, in common with other German military vehicles, normally had up to four types of marking that identified their unit of origin and role. These consisted of national, divisional, tactical and personal markings. The most readily recognizable was the Balkenkreuz, which went through a number of variations as the war progressed.

The cross was usually located on the sides of the superstructure and the tactical number painted onto the turret sides or on the sides of the turret spaced armour (which formed part of the Schürzen: it always lasted longer than the skirt plates which were damaged or torn off whilst the tank was manoeuvring). In Normandy Panzer IVs were photographed with the cross on the forward sides and rear of the turret spaced armour. The three-digit number painted on the turret, usually in black or red lined in white, indicated, left to right, the company number, troop number and lastly the vehicle number.

AUSF D

This Ausf D is finished in the early war standard panzer grey, which in many black and white and colour photographs is very dark and looks almost black. Panzer IVs fought in the initial campaigns on the Western and Eastern Fronts in this colour.

AUSF D

This tank has the Balkenkreuz in black with white outline and the white tactical number 301 on the hull. The side and rear armour was increased from 15mm on the earlier models to 20mm.

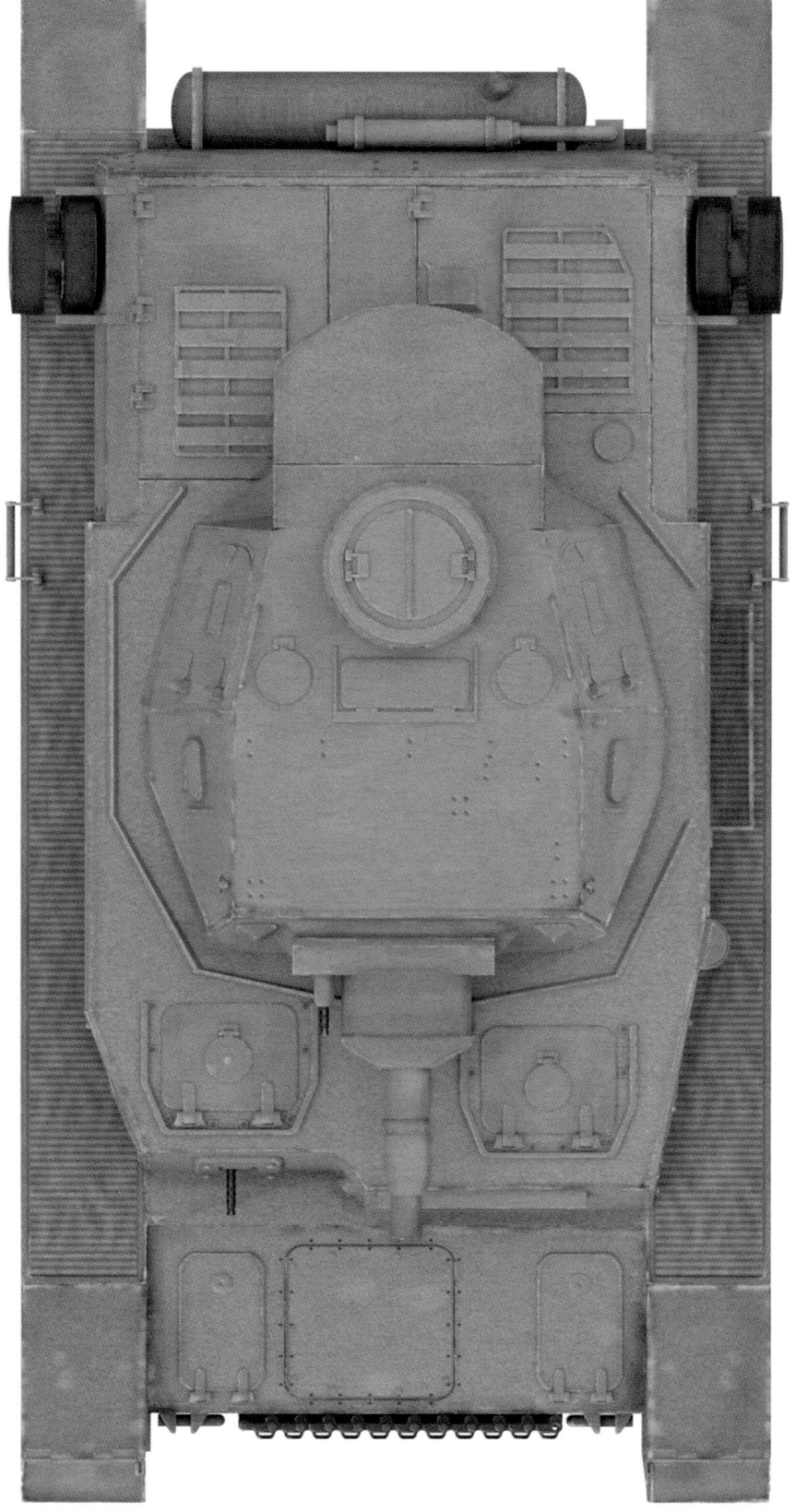

The Ausf D, like the earlier A model, had a distinctive forward-set driver's position visible here from the top view.

AUSF E

The similar-looking Ausf E turret had a redesigned cupola and an exhaust fan vent forward to the right to expel gun fumes. Also the glacis hatches were countersunk level with the glacis plate.

AUSF E

The tank bears the insignia of the 11th Panzer Division which was formed in August 1940. It fought in the Balkans, Russia and France.

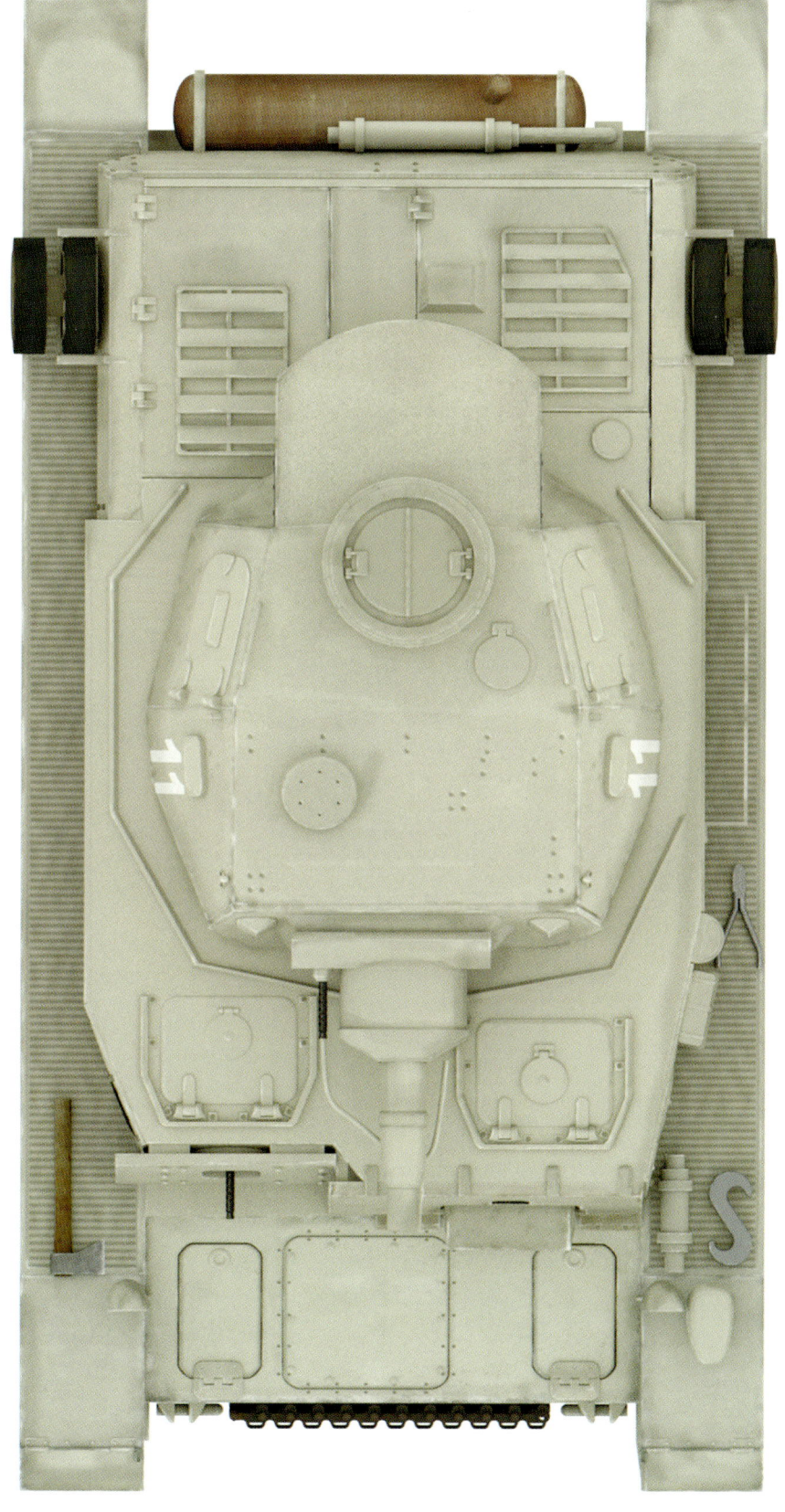

This particular example is finished in dunkel gelb, indicating it had been sent back to the factory for refurbishment.

AUSF F2

This is the upgunned version of the Mk IV armed with the powerful 75mm KwK40 L/43 anti-tank gun, which the British dubbed the 'Pz IV Special.' Bearing the tactical number '444' this F2 belonging to the 21st Panzer Division was photographed in North Africa in 1942. The original image indicates a quite dark base colour. The Afrika Korps swastika and palm tree insignia appeared in a number of slightly different variations.

AUSF F2

Side-on, the F2's gun had a very distinctive circular muzzle brake that made it easy to distinguish from subsequent versions. Also note the ubiquitous Jerry cans that were carried in racks on the sides and at the rear. On some models these side racks were replaced by a bracket for two spare wheels, that also served to up-armour the sides of the fighting compartment.

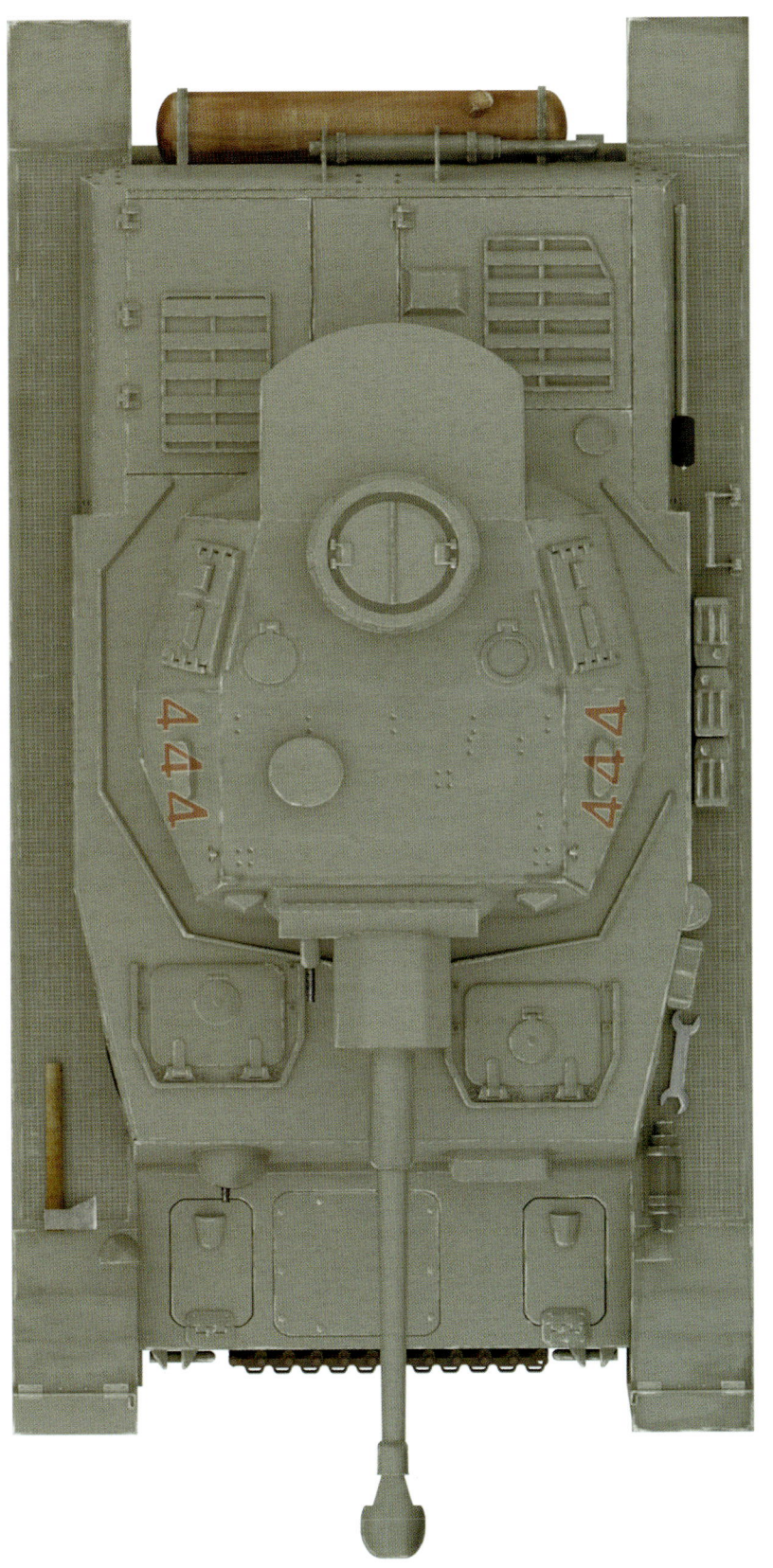

The dunkel gelb has either faded with the weather, dirt and dust or was toned down by the crew for operations in Tunisia during the winter months. Some German vehicles in Libya and Tunisia had a two-tone camouflage pattern. When applied in North Africa the Balkenkreuz was solid white with a black outline or was simply just a white outline.

AUSF G

This formidable-looking Ausf G is fitted with Schürzen on both the turret and hull sides. It is finished in the three-tone camouflage used by the panzers in Normandy during the summer of 1944. The basic dunkel gelb coating has been oversprayed with very irregular patches of oliv grun and rotbraun. Mud and foliage also served to disrupt the outline of the panzers.

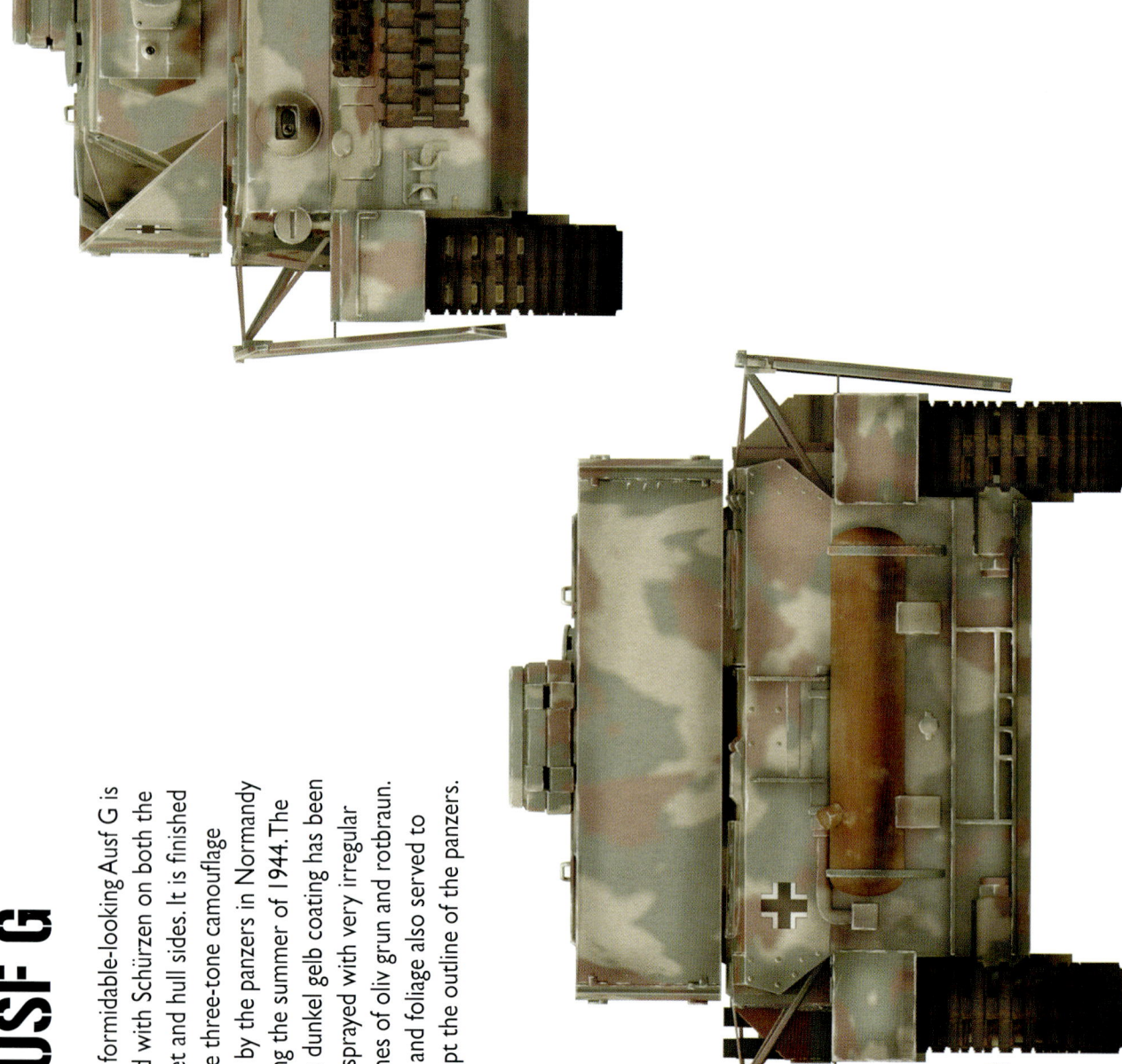

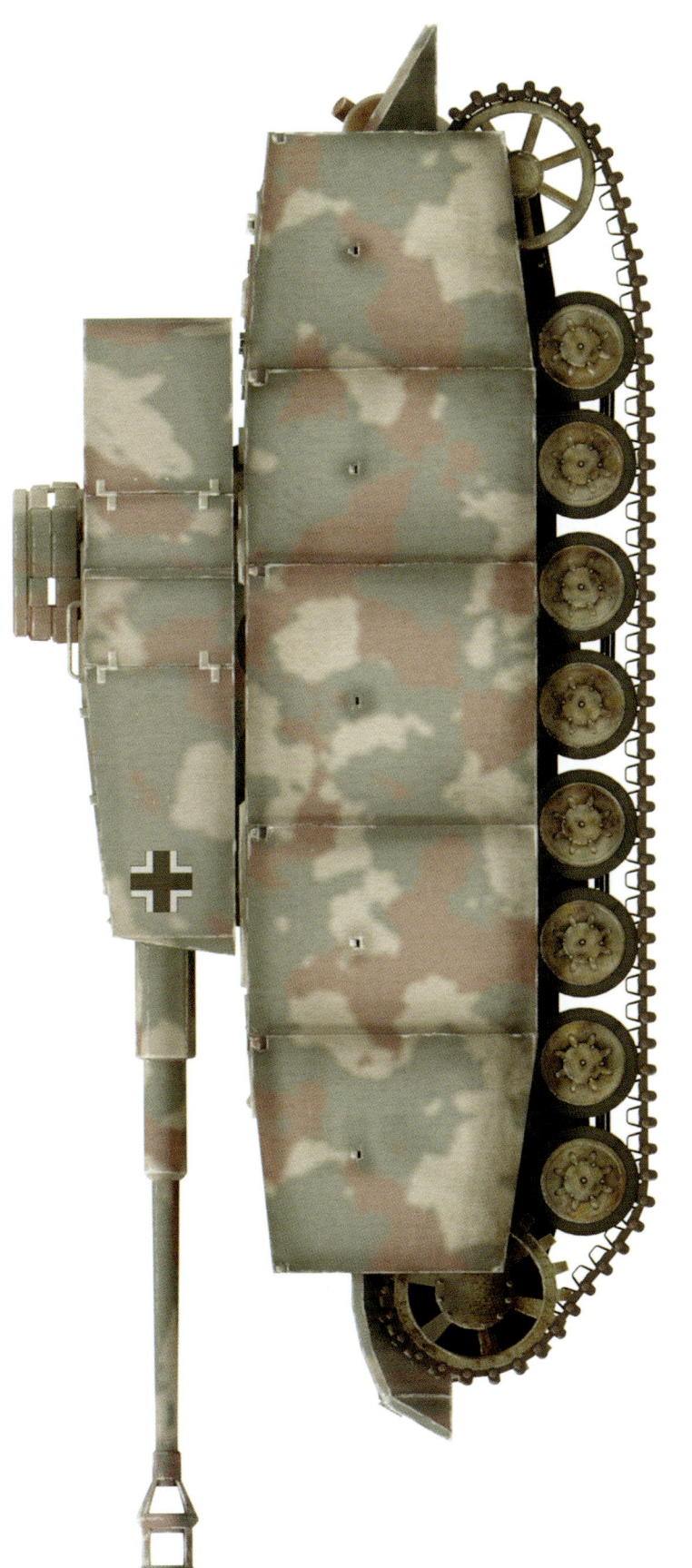

This Ausf G sports the German national cross but lacks a tactical number which was normally applied to the forward edge of the turret Schürzen. Photographic evidence suggests this omission was quite common in the later stages of the war.

AUSF G

This top view shows just how effective the Normandy camouflage was from the air: this was vital in light of the threat posed by Allied fighter-bombers.

Chapter Six

The Rhino and Other Beasts

As well as assault guns and tank destroyers, the Panzer IV chassis was additionally diverted to create a wide variety of self-propelled weapon mounts. These either had anti-tank, anti-aircraft or artillery roles. Key amongst them were the Hornisse (Hornet), Hummel (Bumble Bee), Brummbär (Grizzly Bear) and Möbelwagen (Furniture Van).

Self-Propelled and Support Guns

Hornisse

Work on creating a self-propelled platform for the formidable 88mm Pak43 anti-tank gun started in 1942. This led to the powerful Hornisse (Hornet) that was later called the Nashorn (Rhinoceros). It was decided that this and the Hummel, armed with a 150mm howitzer, would utilize a hybrid Panzer III and IV chassis as a zwischenlösung or interim solution until a dedicated self-propelled gun platform could be designed.

A hybrid prototype was presented to Hitler in October 1942. The Panzer III/IV platform utilized a lengthened Panzer IV hull as the centrepiece of the design. This kept the same basic suspension of four pairs of road wheels and four return rollers except for spacing between the components, while the drive sprocket was that designed for the Panzer III. The glacis plate was extended and on the left-hand side was fitted a small raised armoured compartment for the driver. A circular forward-opening hatch that was set back from the driver's position served the radio operator on the right. This self-propelled mount was known as the Geschützwagen III/IV.

The engine was the same Maybach HL120 used in the Panzer III and IV, giving a 42km/hr speed and a range of 210km. To allow for the open top-fighting compartment at the rear for the 88mm gun crew, the engine was moved to a central position. The compartment was protected on all four sides by slanted armour plates bolted to the hull. These were fairly thin and on the front of the hull amounted to 30mm with just 10mm on the gunshield. The side armour was 10mm on the superstructure and 20mm on the hull.

The initial order with Deutsche-Eisenwerke was for 500 Hornisse, of which 494 were completed between February 1943 and March 1945. After Hitler approved the prototype it was initially agreed to have 100 Hornisse ready by 12 May 1943 in time for his summer offensive and the attack at Kursk. They were first deployed on the Eastern Front with the 655th Heavy Panzerjäger Battalion. Other units equipped with the Hornisse also saw combat on the Western Front and in Italy. Hitler renamed it the Nashorn in 1944.

Hummel

While the Panzer II provided a useful platform for the 105mm field gun it was decided to mount the heavier 150mm howitzer on the Geschützwagen III/IV hybrid chassis. This was to equip the heavy batteries of the self-propelled armoured artillery detachments serving with the panzer and panzergrenadier divisions. At least four different self-propelled howitzer designs utilizing a 105mm gun mounted on the Panzer IV never got much beyond the prototype stage and did not go into full series production.

The 150mm sFH18/1 L/30 was positioned in the middle of the hull over the engine, which resulted in the Hummel having a higher silhouette than the Hornisse. The prototype featured a muzzle brake but this was dispensed with on the production model. Whereas the Hornisse required a four-man crew the Hummel needed six.

Like the Hornisse an order for 100 Hummel was placed with a view to having them ready for the Kursk offensive. Ammunition carriers were also ordered to support the Hummel batteries. To start with, each panzer division only had a single heavy battery equipped with six Hummel plus two ammunition carriers. Later as production increased some had a second heavy battery. Like the Hornisse, the Hummel proved a useful and popular weapon.

Those Hummel built from early 1944 had a crew compartment that extended the initial forward driver's position right across the full width of the hull. In total over 600 had been built by late 1944 with 150 converted into ammunition carriers, as lorries were not up to the job. A variant of the Hummel, known as the Oskette, was produced with wider tracks for the winter fighting on the Eastern Front. German self-propelled guns were not coated in Zimmerit.

Brummbär

Also produced in time for Kursk was the mighty Brummbär assault infantry gun. Alkett developed the Sturmpanzer concept while Krupp modified the Panzer IV chassis to accommodate the 150mm StuH43 L/12 gun (StuH – Sturmhaubitze or assault howitzer). This required a fully enclosed box superstructure for the gunners. Initially the Brummbär utilized fifty-two new Ausf G chassis and eight rebuilt Ausf E and F chassis. Rather than the basic 80mm of armour on the hull front, the first sixty had 50mm plus an additional 50mm armour plate bolted on. The superstructure was also protected by 100mm of armour. Although weighing over 28 tons, the overloaded chassis could still achieve 40km/hr.

The initial production models featured a crude sliding-shutter visor for the driver, similar to that on the Tiger I. The middle production version included a periscope for the driver. Both lacked a close-defence weapon, which left the Brummbär at risk from enemy infantry. Built from April 1944 to the end of the war the final version had a redesigned superstructure armed with a ball-mounted machine gun in the top left-hand corner of the front plate. A cupola was also installed for the commander.

After seeing Alkett's plans in October 1942 Hitler demanded up to sixty Brummbär be ready as soon as possible. On 7 February 1943 it was agreed that forty should be completed in time for Kursk with a follow on order for twenty. The initial production run was conducted during April to May 1943; long-term production was then instigated in November 1943 and lasted until the end of the war. In total 298 Brummbärs were built at Duisburg with another eight converted from Panzer IV gun tanks.

Before leaving the factory all vertical surfaces on the mid-production Brummbär were coated in Zimmerit. Schürzen side skirt armour was also fitted. They were factory-sprayed in dunkel gelb, and areas were then oversprayed with small patches of diluted oliv grun. The first unit to deploy the Brummbär was the 216th Sturmpanzer Battalion, which fought at Kursk and was involved in the defensive battles near Zaparozhye ending in October 1943. Three other battalions were formed fighting on the Eastern and Western Fronts as well as in Italy.

Assault Guns and Tank Destroyers

From late 1943 the Panzer IV chassis was also used as the basis for a series of turretless assault guns and tank destroyers. These consisted of the Sturmgeschütz IV, Jagdpanzer IV and the Panzer IV/70. Combined these represented some 3,120 vehicles with roughly a thousand of each type. These are noteworthy because they diverted valuable tank production just as the tide was turning to what were essentially defensive rather than offensive operations. Their lack of turret and very limited traverse with the hull-mounted main gun naturally limited their tactical flexibility.

Sturmgeschütz IV, Jagdpanzer IV and Panzer IV/70*

The StuG IV first went into production in December 1943 and continued until the end of the war. As a result Krupp-Gruson completely abandoned building Panzer IV gun tanks. The Vomag Jagdpanzer IV was only built during 1944 and overlapped with the Panzer IV/70(V), which remained in production until March 1945.

While Vomag also discontinued Panzer IV gun tank manufacture, Nibelungenwerke built both Ausf J gun tanks and chassis for the Panzer IV/70 until the very end. Notably, the Panzer IV/70(A) built by Nibelungenwerke was a stopgap model using chassis intended for gun tank production. As a result the chassis did not have a modified nose, which meant mounting the superstructure half a metre higher than that on the Jagdpanzer IV and the Panzer IV/70(V).

Self-Propelled Flak Guns

Growing Allied air superiority by 1943 made it increasingly necessary for the Germans to divert a greater proportion of their armoured fighting vehicle production to the output of anti-aircraft tanks or flakpanzers. By 1944 the panzer divisions were in need of fully-tracked armoured anti-aircraft guns that could accompany them into combat. This requirement resulted in the Möbelwagen (Furniture Van), Ostwind (East Wind) and Wirbelwind (Whirlwind), all employing the Panzer IV chassis. These were issued to the anti-aircraft platoons of the panzer regiments. The Möbelwagen was by far the most numerous.

Möbelwagen

The Möbelwagen was armed with a 37mm FlaK43 L/60 anti-aircraft gun, with the chassis supplied by Krupp-Gruson, and it proved quite successful. The FlaK43 was designed to replace the earlier FlaK37, which used a two-wheeled trailer similar to the 20mm FlaK30. This newer gun featured a FlaK37 body but also had a gas-actuated

---

* These are covered in greater detail in *German Assault Guns and Tank Destroyers 1940–1945*.

mechanism from an aircraft cannon replacing the original recoil-actuated mechanism. This almost doubled the rate of fire. Its effective ceiling was 4,200m. The gun was also mounted in a twin configuration with one gun above the other, rather than the more usual side-by-side. This double configuration was not tried on the Möbelwagen as it would have left the crew permanently exposed apart from the gun shield.

On the Möbelwagen a fighting compartment for the gunners was created by a simple four-sided 50mm plate superstructure, which could be lowered to a horizontal position to permit the gun to traverse 360° at low elevation. The hull had 80mm of armour and the superstructure 50mm. Between March 1944 and March the following year some 240 Möbelwagen were produced by Deutsche-Eisenwerke. It does not appear that the Möbelwagen hull was given an application of Zimmerit on leaving the factory.

Wirbelwind

Whereas the Möbelwagen only had a flat, largely exposed platform for the gun, the Wirbelwind was equipped with an open-topped turret into which was mounted a 20mm Flakvierling 38 quad. The turret offered just 16mm of armour. This anti-aircraft gun was an improvement on the 20mm FlaK30, which had seen action in Spain and was deployed on a two-wheeled trailer. The rate of fire was increased from 280 to 420 rounds per minute. The Flakvierling 38 was then tried as twin guns and finally a quad mounting was adopted, capable of firing 1,680 shells per minute. The gun's ceiling was 2,000m.

The Wirbelwind was designed to supplement Möbelwagen production by using existing Panzer IV chassis that had been returned from the front for factory repair. From July to November 1944 Ostbau converted just eighty-six Wirbelwind before the use of the inadequate 20mm gun was abandoned in favour of the 37mm gun.

Ostwind

Trials were held in July 1944 mounting a 37mm FlaK43 gun in a turret similar to that used on the Wirbelwind. This resulted in the Ostwind, comprising a six-sided open-top turret on a converted Panzer IV chassis. An order for 100 was placed with Ostbau on 18 August 1944 but by the end of the war they had produced just thirty-six conversions.

The majority of the Flakpanzer IV were deployed to the Eastern Front, though some Möbelwagen saw action in France in 1944. Wirbelwind and Ostwind flak panzers saw combat during Hitler's Ardennes offensive in December 1944 and were also used in a ground support role. Both these type of Flakpanzer IV had their hulls finished with Zimmerit.

It had been planned to replace the Ostwind and Möbelwagen with the Panzer IV-based Kugelblitz, armed with twin 30mm guns. Just two Kugelblitz were ever completed, so seven new chassis earmarked for the project were also used to produce Ostwind. Ostbau was looking to produce an Ostwind II armed with two 37mm guns and a Flakpanzer IV armed with a 30mm quad, but loss of their facilities ensured this did not happen.

Support Vehicles

As well as being diverted for self-propelled guns and tanks destroyers, the Panzer IV chassis was employed in a wide range of command and support roles.

Command Tank

The Panzer III was likewise deployed in a very large variety of roles, including the Panzerbefehlswagen or command vehicle and the Panzerbeobachtungswagen or artillery observation post vehicle. Hundreds of these were produced but by 1944 they were increasingly in short supply due to the end of Panzer III gun tank production. To make up the shortfall the German Army had little choice but to convert existing Panzer IVs to Panzerbefehlswagen mit 7.5cm KwK L/48.

About half the Panzer III command vehicles did not have a main gun in order to create extra workspace. None of the Panzer III observation vehicles had their main gun. This meant they were reliant on a single machine gun for protection and were at risk if they got too close to the front. In contrast the Panzer IV command vehicle retained its 75mm gun.

From March to September 1944 Nibelungenwerke converted some ninety-seven Mk IVs to a command role. This primarily involved the installation of the FuG5 (10-watt transmitter) and FuG7 or the FuG8 radios (20- and 30-watt transmitters respectively). These were the standard tank, ground-to-air and divisional link sets. The FuG5 aerial along with a TSR1 1.4m high periscope was fixed to the turret top. The distinctive star antenna for the FuG7/8 was attached to the rear of the hull on the right-hand edge of the tail plate. These command tanks were issued to Panzer IV battalions.

Observation Tank

The artillery observation post vehicle was essentially the same but with different radio equipment, comprising the FuG4 and FuG8. This provided an artillery-control set and a divisional link. This conversion work was conducted by Nibelungenwerke but started slightly later, although it involved similar quantities of tanks. A total of ninety Panzer IVs were converted into Panzerbeobachtungswagen IV from July 1944 to March 1945. These were issued to the Hummel batteries.

Submersible Tank

Like the Panzer III, a number of Mk IVs were converted into submersible tanks known as Tauchpanzer in mid-1940. This was done in preparation for Hitler's Operation Sealion, the proposed invasion of England. In theory it allowed the panzers to operate in water up to 15m deep. Whilst almost 170 Tauchpanzer III were produced there were just forty-two Tauchpanzer IV conversions.

This comprised fitting the air-intakes with locking covers and the exhausts with non-return valves replacing the normal mufflers. Also waterproof fabric covers were applied to the hull machine gun, the gun mantlet and the cupola. An inflatable rubber tube encompassed the turret ring. A specially-designed metal cover with a vision block made the driver's visor watertight. A pipe suspended from a floating snorkel connected to the back of the tank allowed it to draw air when submerged and a gyrocompass facilitated underwater navigation.

Trials and training showed that the Tauchpanzer was a reasonable successful innovation. When Hitler finally abandoned Sealion they were made redundant. Nevertheless, the Tauchpanzers did not go to waste as they were shipped to Milowitz near Prague in the spring of 1941 and prepared for another mission. Most of them had a long rigid snorkel attached to the commander's cupola, making them capable of deep river crossings. These Tauchpanzers took part in Operation Barbarossa with the 18th Panzer Division in June 1941.

Bridge-layer

During the 1930s the emphasis on fixed fortifications in Europe resulted in the German Inspectorate of Engineers concluding that there was a strong requirement for an armoured bridge layer. Early experiments utilizing the Panzer I and II were soon abandoned as they could not carry a large-enough tank bridge. Instead they came up with the Brückenleger IV.

Four Panzer IV Ausf C chassis were assigned for conversion in August 1939. The following month an additional 16 Ausf D chassis were requisitioned. By January 1940 it was anticipated that twelve BL IV would be delivered with two employing a Krupp-designed bridge and the rest using a Magirus development. One had a forward-pivoting gantry while the other slid the bridge into position horizontally.

The original order had been for fifty 9m bridges, but this was cut by thirty so a new design could be fitted to sixty Panzer IVs. Experience in France and the Low Countries showed there was actually little call for the services of the BL IV and the programme was cancelled. During 1940–41 it was decided to restore fifteen BL IV to a gun tank role. In the end just twenty bridgelayers were issued to five panzer divisions.

Infantry Assault Bridge

There was another design that employed a 50m extending bridge using Panzer IV Ausf C chassis. Known as the Infanterie Sturmsteg or infantry assault bridge, this Magirus construction comprised two bridges side-by-side that created beams for a walkway very similar to a fire-fighting ladder. Just two Sturmsteg were completed in February 1940 and saw use in the invasion of France. One was disabled, losing its tracks and several road wheels. No further conversions were carried out.

Armoured Recovery Vehicle

Late in the war a very limited number of Bergepanzer IV or recovery vehicles were produced to support the panzer divisions. This was a fairly crude affair and consisted of replacing the turret with a wooden box-body on top of the fighting compartment for the mechanics. Mountings were also installed on the rear engine deck to take a derrick crane for engine lifting. Just thirty-six Bergepanzer IV were converted from October 1944 to December 1944.

In contrast 150 Bergepanzer III were produced during that same year as the Panzer III had outlived its usefulness by this stage. Instructions were that all Mk IIIs being returned from the front for maintenance were to be converted to a recovery role. It is likely that others were produced unofficially as field conversions from damaged tanks or those under repair. Both types of Bergepanzer were issued to Panzer IV and StuG III/IV workshop companies.

Hummel Ammunition Carrier

Externally the Hummel ammunition carrier differed from the Hummel, simply by having its gun removed and the resulting gap plated over. Internally the fighting compartment was converted to allow for extra ammunition stowage. These vehicles were produced both in the factory and frequently as field conversions.

Karl Mortar Ammunition Carrier

During the winter of 1940 and the summer of 1941 the Germans produced six Karlgerät, which were enormous 600mm self-propelled super-heavy siege mortars. These required tracked ammunition carriers and in October 1939 a brand-new Panzer Ausf D chassis was used as a prototype. A new superstructure was constructed, while over the engine compartment were fitted racks that could take four massive 600mm rounds. To get these rounds to the mortar a crane was installed on the front right-hand side of the superstructure.

Once green-lighted it was decided in 1941 to use a newer model Panzer IV and 13 Ausf F1 chassis were converted to Munitionsschlepper für Karlgerät. A number of rebuilt Panzer IV chassis were also pressed into service. These carriers saw action in support of the mortars on the Eastern Front, most memorably during the siege of Sevastopol in 1942.

The Hornisse self-propelled heavy anti-tank gun was a hybrid using components from the Panzer III and IV. Armament comprised the powerful 88mm PaK43/1 L/71 gun which was far too large to mount in a conventional tank turret.

This shot shows how the main armament on the Hornisse made it nose-heavy and difficult to manoeuvre in anything other than open spaces. The gun's long range made it ideal for the open Russian steppe.

The armour protecting the gunners' fighting compartment on the Hornisse was very poor, amounting to just 10mm. Nonetheless, this tank killer proved very successful and almost 500 had been built by the end of the war.

The Hummel, like the Hornisse, first appeared in the summer of 1943. This self-propelled gun carried the 150mm sFH18/1 l/30 howitzer. The early production models built in 1943 had a raised armoured forward driving compartment.

A direct hit destroyed this final-model Hummel in Berlin in April 1945. The two blurred bands round the barrel near the muzzle suggest it was being using in an anti-tank role.

A crew of five gunners and a driver were required to operate the Hummel. This is a 1944 model as the superstructure front plate for the driver and radio operator are flush.

A 1944–5 model Hummel captured by the Red Army in Budapest, Hungary in 1945. The superstructure and gun shield on the Hummel only had 10mm of armour. The hull front had 30mmm with just 20mm on the sides and rear.

The remains of two Brummbär numbered '222' and '110' captured at the end of the war. Both appear to have been incomplete as their drive sprockets are missing. Almost 300 Sturmpanzer IV were built.

Both Brummbär were fitted with rails to hold the Schürzen. The commander's cupola and machine-gun ball mount at the front identifies them as late-production models.

The requirement for tracked anti-aircraft guns to support the panzers resulted in the Möbelwagen. This consisted of a 37mm FlaK43 L/60 anti-aircraft gun mounted on a turretless Panzer IV chassis.

The sides of the fighting compartment folded down on the Möbelwagen to allow full 360° traverse.

A Möbelwagen getting the once-over from curious American troops. The gun shield offered just 25mm of protection but the fighting compartment front plate that is folded down was 50mm thick.

The Wirbelwind was produced to supplement the Möbelwagen. Its armament consisted of a 20mm Flakvierling 38 quad, but this was not as effective against low-flying fighter-bombers as the 37mm gun. These well-camouflaged examples were keen not to attract attention to themselves while on the move.

The hull and superstructure of this Wirbelwind has been coated in the anti-magnetic Zimmerit paste.

Two Wirbelwind captured on the Western Front during the winter of 1944–5. Less than 100 were built during the second half of 1944 as it was intended to replace them with the Ostwind armed with the FlaK43.

To support the invasion of England in 1940 the Germans produced the Tauchpanzer or submersible tank. Only forty-two Tauchpanzer IV conversions were ever produced and these were involved in the attack on the Soviet Union.

A number of Panzer IV bridgelayer variants were produced including twenty Brückenleger IV and two Infanterie Sturmsteg, one of which is seen here.

The Infanterie Sturmsteg took part in the invasion of France in 1940 where this one was disabled. The Germans abandoned their Panzer IV bridgelayer concept shortly after.

Chapter Seven

In the Desert and Mountains

On the eve of the Second World War Hitler's Wehrmacht had just over 3,300 tanks, of which only 629 were Panzer III and IV. By May 1940 every tank detachment had a medium tank company of six to eleven Panzer IVs. When the invasion of France and the Low Countries commenced there were 280 Ausf A, B, C and D Mk IVs equipping the panzer divisions. After the defeat of France some of these were sent to North Africa to help the Italians.

When the armoured units of Rommel's Deutsches Afrika Korps (DAK) arrived in Libya they were equipped with the Panzer IV Ausf C and D and then later the Ausf E and F1, armed with the 75mm KwK L/24 gun that fired the same high-explosive projectile as the Ausf F2 (dubbed the Panzer IV 'Special' by the British) equipped with the L/43.

The first elements of DAK landed in Tripoli on 14 February 1941 with the disembarkation of the 3rd Reconnaissance Battalion, 5th Light Division; other units, most notably two battalions of the 5th Panzer Regiment, followed. The 5th and 8th Panzer Regiments initially took just forty Ausf D and E Mk IVs to North Africa. These regiments formed the spearhead of the 21st and 15th Panzer Divisions respectively.

Significantly, the most common Panzer IV were the Ausf D, E and F1 which made up around 25 per cent of Rommel's armoured formations. Armed with the short 75mm KwK37 L/24 gun, they were inferior to the later 50mm gun of the Panzer III. Prior to the Crusader battles in November 1941 the British were able to field 748 tanks armed with 40mm or 37mm high-velocity guns against 248 panzers, of which 174 were Panzer III and IVs, the rest being Panzer IIs with a 20mm gun. The Italians supported Rommel with 146 inferior tanks that were armed with a low-velocity 47mm gun. What really gave Rommel an advantage was his superior tactics.

In the summer of 1942 he began to receive the up-gunned F2 armed with the long-barrelled 75mm KwK40 L/43 gun. This could punch through 85mm of armour at 1,000 yards and was superior to the British 2-pounder (40mm) and 6-pounder (57mm) and the American-supplied M3 Grant's 75mm gun. Luckily for the British the Germans had only received twenty-seven Panzer IV F2s by August 1942, which they employed to spearhead Rommel's counteroffensive. Despite their presence Rommel's attack at Alam Halfa was held.

Crucially the F2 was never available in sufficient numbers, with around thirty with each of DAK's panzer divisions at any one time compared to 100 Mk IIIs. While its gun could penetrate all British and American armour at a distance and more arrived between August and October 1942, they were nothing like the quantities of tanks reaching the British 8th Army prior to El Alamein. Some Ausf G also fought with the Germans in Tunisia.

British armour could cope with the Panzer I and II but not the subsequent two models. The Panzer III armed with a 50mm gun was superior to any Allied armour until 1942 and the arrival of the M3 Grant. The early Mk IV with its short 75mm gun was able to fire armour piercing, high explosive and smoke so could outshoot very vulnerable British cruiser tanks and shell exposed 25-pounder gun crews.

British cruiser tanks, as well as the Matilda and Valentine infantry support tanks armed with the 2-pounder gun, could only fire armour piercing rounds. Initially the 6-pounder installed on the Crusader and the Churchill was only intended to fire armour piercing. While the Panzer IV could fire from 3,000 yards with HE, British tanks had to wait for them to close to within 1,000–500 yards to engage with their solid AP shot: in the meantime their exposed artillery would have to retreat.

The Panzer III and Panzer IV F2 therefore had little trouble dealing with their opponents. British cruiser tanks such as the Mk II and IV had a maximum of 30mm of armour, while the Mk I and III were even more lightly armoured at just 14mm. The Mk VI Crusader was little better – with the final production version the Crusader III sporting 51mm of armour. It was also up-gunned to the British 6-pounder. The Matilda and Valentine had a respectable maximum of 78mm and 65mm respectively but like all British tanks were slower than the panzers and under-gunned. The Grant and Sherman had 37mm and 75mm armour respectively.

Against the F2 the Grant was not only disadvantaged by its gun, but also by the mounting the weapon in the hull instead of a fully revolving turret. This meant it could not fight dug-in from a 'hull-down' position when on the defensive. Likewise the Grant's high silhouette exposed the top of the tank to enemy fire when on the offensive. The Panzer IV also proved more than a match for the Sherman in North Africa.

Ultimately though, the Panzer III and IV were overwhelmed by superior numbers and air power. Hitler never adequately reinforced his troops in North Africa until it was far too late and they were trapped. Despite the effectiveness of the Panzer IV F2 and the introduction of a few Tigers, particularly against the inexperienced American army, capitulation was inevitable. The very last of the Panzer IVs were disabled by Allied bombers – one of which was photographed on 10 May 1943 just two days before the Axis surrendered in Tunisia.

Similarly, significant numbers of Panzer IVs were never available in Italy. German panzer divisions were always thin on the ground during the Italian campaign. Generally German infantry divisions relied on the support of panzergrenadier units, which had fewer armoured fighting vehicles than the regular panzer divisions and relied on assault guns, not tanks.

The key tank unit was the 26th Panzer Division, which transferred to Italy in 1943 and remained there for the rest of the war until its surrender near Bologna in May 1945. The 16th Panzer Division only fought in Italy for six months between June and November 1943 seeing action at Salerno and Naples before being sent to the Eastern Front. These divisions were equipped with the Panzer IV Ausf G, H and J.

The Luftwaffe also fielded the Panzer IV in Italy. The Hermann Göring Panzer Division, which had been destroyed in Tunisia, was reformed in southern Italy and Sicily and played a key role in the Sicilian campaign in July and August 1943. Escaping to the Italian mainland following the Allied landings on the island it was given the title Fallschirm Panzer Division Hermann Göring, although the Fallschirm (Parachute) designation was purely honorary. The Parachute Panzer Regiment Hermann Göring included a panzer and assault gun battalion.

A British Crusader passes a burning Panzer IV during Operation Crusader on 27 November 1941. British tank armament, comprising the 2-pounder gun, was wholly inadequate against the Panzer III and IV.

Another shot of the burning Panzer IV. The most common models in North Africa were the Ausf D, E and F1, all armed with the close-support short 75mm gun.

Panzer IV '618' belonging to the 1st SS Panzer Division in Milan during September 1943 following the German occupation of Italy.

British troops sheltering by two burning Panzer IVs caught on the road near Salerno on 22 September 1943, following the landings on the Italian mainland.

Men hurry past the same tanks. Both have the turret Schürzen but the side plates are missing.

A battery of Hornisse self-propelled anti-tank guns near Anzio, Italy in 1944.

Brümmbar Sturmpanzer IV during the battle for Anzio. The Brümmbar also saw action on the Western and Eastern Fronts. This particular example has lost the central plate on the left-hand skirt.

This Ausf G was photographed near Lucera in Italy on 27 October 1943. It was being used for weapons tests by the British 8th Army.

This Panzer IV Ausf H was destroyed near Salerno, Italy. The engine compartment and hull have been badly damaged by an explosion.

Chapter Eight

From Barbarossa to Berlin

Those short-barrel Panzer IVs lost during the invasion of the Soviet Union in the summer of 1941 were replaced by the spring of 1942, but crucially there was no increase in overall numbers. However, the Red Army's T-34 tank, with a maximum of 70mm frontal armour, was now vulnerable to the recently-introduced Panzer IV Ausf F2. Even at 1,000 yards its 75mm Kwk40 L/43 could penetrate 87mm of armour and the subsequent Panzer IV Ausf G and H were both armed with the more powerful Kwk40 L/48. They finally gave the Panzerwaffe parity.

Nonetheless in terms of tank production the Germans could not compete, in November 1942 they managed just 100 Panzer IVs compared to 1,000 Soviet T-34s. The following month, rather than retool for the Panzer IV, the Panzer III assembly lines were turned over to StuG III assault gun production. Following Hitler's major summer offensive in 1942, by early 1943 the eighteen panzer divisions on the Eastern Front had less than 600 tanks. This did not bode well for his Kursk offensive. However, Hitler managed to gather 1,850 panzers supported by 200 obsolete tanks and over 530 assault guns. Along with the Panzer IV, the Panzer III provided the bulk of Hitler's armour employed during Operation Citadel. The Panther, making its debut, was in short supply, as was the Tiger.

Also making their debut at Kursk in July 1943 were the Panzer IV-based Hummel and Hornisse. While the latter had a very effective anti-tank gun it was really a defensive rather than offensive armoured fighting vehicle. The numbers available though were once again a problem. Both had only gone into production in early 1943, with about 100 of each type ready for the summer. The Hummel units were supported by obsolete Panzer IIs equipped with radios to act as command and observation tanks. Also to help smash Soviet fortifications were sixty-six newly-built Brummbär comprising a short 150mm howitzer mounted on a Panzer IV chassis.

Despite their best efforts the Panzer IV, and the newly-introduced Panther and Tiger, were simply swamped at Kursk by a well-prepared and more numerous enemy. Hitler had been warned he was outnumbered but refused to give ground or let the initiative pass to the Red Army so had chosen to attack first with dire results. The panzers were crushed in a massive tank battle at Prokhorovka. Hitler lost around 1,600 panzers of which 300 were irreparable losses.

Although the Panzer IV remained the German workhorse on the Eastern Front, the earlier Ausf D, E and F armed with the short 75mm gun were completely phased out through attrition in early 1944. The panzer divisions were equipped with the newer F2, G and H variants, although they were in danger of being outclassed by some of the newer heavily-armed Soviet armour.

In the summer of 1944 Hitler had too few Panzer IVs supporting Army Group Centre that was holding the exposed frontline in Byelorussia. The army group under Field Marshal Ernst Busch was predominantly equipped with assault guns. Busch's only unit with Panzer IVs, that constituted his sole reserve, was the 20th Panzer Division. Army Group North was little better off with just the 12th Panzer Division equipped with Mk IVs. The two Army Groups in Ukraine were much stronger with fourteen panzer divisions but this was where Hitler was anticipating Stalin would strike.

Stalin conducted a major offensive to liberate Minsk and Byelorussia in late June 1944. General Jordan, commanding the German 9th Army, sought and received Busch's permission to commit the 20th Panzer Division to try and stem the Soviet tide. The division could muster seventy Panzer IVs, its other panzer battalion being busy re-equipping with Panthers. At that very moment General Batov's 65th Army broke through on the southern approaches to Bobruisk and General Rokossovsky committed the 1st Guards Tank Corps to exploit the breach. A dithering Jordan ordered 20th Panzer to retrace its tracks and head south, bumping into the Soviets near Slobodka south of Bobruisk.

It rapidly became apparent that not only was German-held Bobruisk under threat but also those German divisions still east of the Berezina River. By 26 June the battered 20th Panzer had been driven back to the city with the Soviet 9th Tank Corps bearing down on it from the east and the Soviet 1st Guards Tank Corps from the south. The 1st Guards Tank Corps cut the roads from Bobruisk to the north and north-west on the night of 26/27 June, closing the trap.

The 5th Panzer Division was moved up from Kovel to defensive positions east of Borisov with a view to covering those troops withdrawing from Mogilev, which had been overrun late on the 27th. Under General Karl Decker, 5th Panzer began to arrive in Minsk on 26 June with the all-but-impossible task of holding the Moscow-Minsk Highway. The division was equipped with just fifty-five Panzer IVs and seventy Panthers, supported by Captain von Beschwitz's twenty-nine Tiger Is of Heavy Panzer Battalion 505. Their first mission was to put a stop line in place north-east of Borisov. Like 20th Panzer, they too failed to stem the Red Army's tidal wave.

The year was a complete disaster for Hitler and those regiments equipped with the Panzer IV. Throughout 1944 Hitler lost 2,640 Panzer IVs on the Eastern Front. This was more than could be replaced. The previous year he had suffered losses of 2,350 Panzer IVs, with some divisions down to as few as twelve tanks. The no-frills Panzer IV Ausf J which appeared in mid-1944 was the final production model and was greatly simplified to speed construction. However, the manual turret traverse was not greatly liked by the crews. Production ran until March 1945 by which time less than 2,000 had been produced. It was not enough

Reportedly 287 Panzer IVs were lost on the Eastern Front during January 1945. Within months the Red Army was poised before the very gates of Berlin and victory. By this stage the German armies tasked with protecting the capital had very few panzers left. In total it is estimated that the Red Army accounted for 6,150 Panzer IVs or about 75 per cent of all Panzer IV losses during the war.

Whitewashed short-barrelled Panzer IVs on the road to Moscow. The bad weather and Red Army counter-attacks ensured they did not capture the city.

Those early-model Ausf C, D and E lost during the invasion of Russia were replaced by the up-gunned Ausf F2 and G during the spring of 1942.

A Soviet soldier examines a knocked-out Panzer IV Ausf H in the summer of 1943.

This illustrates the extent to which the Schürzen greatly enhanced the protection of the Panzer IV's hull and turret. The side plates, though, were invariably lost and once damaged were often not replaced. These show signs of impact marks.

Ausf G/H serving in Russia. Although both tanks have the brackets for the side plates only the turret Schürzen remains. The nearest tank bears the tactical number '325'.

Hummels being shipped to the front. The self-propelled mounting known as the Geschützwagen III/IV proved highly successful with the Hummel and Hornisse.

The Hummel, like the Hornisse, made its debut in the summer of 1943 at Kursk, where it served in the heavy batteries of the armoured artillery detachments with the panzer divisions. The exposed crew had no protection from indirect fire.

A Hornisse camouflaged for operations during the Russian winter. Renamed the Nashorn in 1944 it stayed in production until the end of the war, although the Jagdpanzer IV and Panzer IV/70 took priority. The Hornisse made its first appearance at Kursk. Its powerful and long-ranged 88mm gun meant it could kill Soviet tanks at great distances – this helped cancel out the risks caused by its high profile and light armour.

These Hornisse belong to the 519th Heavy Panzerjäger Battalion serving on the Eastern Front in the winter of 1944. This was one of six such battalions equipped with this Panzer IV-based tank destroyer.

A Panzer IV Ausf H on the Eastern Front with its Schürzen intact. It bears the tactical number '505' and has a two-tone camouflage scheme.

Hummel belonging to the 1st SS Panzer Division being transported by rail. Tarpaulins have been fitted to keep the rain out of the fighting compartment. The key and shield divisional insignia can just be seen on the front of the superstructure on the right-hand side.

Chapter Nine

Beyond the Seine

The Panzer IV played a significant part in the Battle for Normandy. The most common type of panzer resisting the Allies in occupied France in 1944 was the Panzer IV Ausf H and Ausf J totalling around 750 tanks. Around two-thirds of the Panzer IV battalions were armed with the Ausf H and the rest with the newer Ausf J. With frontal armour of 80mm and the 75mm KwK 40 L/48 anti-tank gun, the Panzer IV provided the fighting backbone of the ten panzer divisions deployed to France (in all five army and five Waffen-SS divisions fielded it in Normandy).

It, along with the Panther and Tiger tanks, gave the Germans a distinct advantage in tank-to-tank engagements during the battles in the Normandy bocage. Notably its gun had a 20 per cent higher muzzle velocity than that of the ubiquitous American-built M4 Sherman's 75mm gun, meaning it could punch through 92mm of armour at 500 yards, while the Sherman could only manage 68mm. In addition the Panzer IV proved remarkably reliable, maintaining consistently good operational rates.

Normally the Panzer IV was allocated to the 2nd Battalion or II Abteilung of a panzer regiment, while the 1st was equipped with the Panther, although there were a number of exceptions in France. In the case of the 9th Panzer Division the 1st Battalion of its Panzer Regiment 33 was equipped with Panzer IVs and both battalions of 21st Panzer's Panzer Regiment 22 were equipped with it.

At the beginning of June 1944 the 2nd Panzer Division, deployed east of the Seine at the start of the campaign, had a total of ninety-eight Panzer IVs on its strength. By early July the division still had eighty-five of them in the field with another eleven in the workshop. The 9th Panzer Division, based in the south of France, arrived in the Normandy in early August with a total of eighty-two Panzer IVs.

The 21st Panzer Division, already in Normandy from the start, had a total of 104 Panzer IVs, including six old Ausf G and six even older Ausf B or C with the short 75mm gun. None of the latter seems to have been upgraded and lacked Zimmerit and Schürzen. Before D-Day one of the Ausf B/C dubbed 'Heidi' was photographed in St Martin de Fresnay, south-east of St Pierre-sur-Dives, where its crew were happily shopping for Camembert cheese. It is not clear if this was an authorized use of official military equipment or simply a PR exercise.

On 24 May 1944 another fourteen Panzer IVs were despatched to 21st Panzer, but it is unlikely that they had arrived by early June. During the battle for Normandy another thirty were sent to the division including three command tanks. The final ten gun tanks probably did not arrive in time to take part in the fighting.

Panzer *Lehr* Division, initially north-west of Orleans, had ninety-nine Panzer IVs. It was sent another eleven Mk IVs as replacements on 8 July 1944. Following heavy fighting with the Americans, by 22 August the division had just ten left. When the 116th Panzer Division *Windhund*, north of Paris, was committed to the battle for Normandy in late July it had 86 Panzer IVs. Its other armoured fighting vehicles include three older Panzer IVs with the short 75mm gun. Following the German retreat and the fighting at St Lambert the division was only able to retrieve four Panzer IVs from the battlefield.

The Waffen-SS panzer divisions committed to Normandy were also equipped with the Panzer IV. The 1st SS Panzer Division *Leibstandarte Adolf Hitler*, east of Brussels, mustered forty-two Panzer IVs in its 1st Tank Battalion. A further eight were in for repair. Deliveries during June amounted to another fifty-three tanks. After being sent to Normandy by late July the division was able to field sixty-one Panzer IVs.

The 2nd SS Panzer Division *Das Reich* by the beginning of June had fifty-four Panzer IVs, of which ten were in the workshop. Further deliveries of armour meant that the 2nd SS was to field a total of eighty-three Panzer IVs, which included the newer Ausf J. Many of these were lost in the Roncey pocket at the end of July, though some of the Mk IVs from 2nd SS managed to escape.

The 9th SS Panzer Division *Hohenstaufen* had forty-eight Panzer IVs at the start of the campaign, but seven of these were in the shop. Its sister division 10th SS *Frundsberg* was able to deploy thirty-nine and by mid-August had only lost twelve. However, just eight Panzer IVs were available to hold the Americans at bay. The formidable 12th SS *Hitlerjugend* had an authorized strength of 101 Panzer IVs though only ninety-one were combat ready. By 10 August after much heavy fighting the division had just fifteen left.

By 1944 the panzer divisions were largely relying on flak guns mounted on half-tracks for air defence, including the SdKfz 10/4 and SdKfz 7/1. In Normandy the Flakpanzer 38(t) using Czech-built chassis was in service instead of the Flakpanzer IV with the 2nd, 9th, Panzer *Lehr* and 1st SS Panzer Divisions. In theory eight Flakpanzer IV Möbelwagen were allocated to the anti-aircraft section of a panzer regiments headquarters' company. In July 1944 (on paper at least) Möbelwagens were assigned to the 12th SS and 116th Panzer Divisions. Very limited numbers of Wirbelwind also saw combat in Normandy.

The lack of infantry divisions, which were held north of the Seine, meant the panzers bore the brunt of the fighting. By the beginning of July 1944 the unrelenting operational commitment of the panzers had taken its toll: 42 per cent of the Panzer IVs and 58 per cent of the Panthers were in the maintenance depots. Prior to Montgomery's Goodwood offensive on 18 July Panzer IVs of 21st Panzer along with Tiger tanks from Heavy Panzer Battalion 503 were caught in the Allied saturation bombing near Château de Manneville 10km east of Caen. The effects were devastating, with tanks simply tossed upside-down like they were toys. From a force of about fifty panzers over half were lost, many others suffering mechanical failures.

Although Goodwood failed to breakthrough the incredibly tough German defences it contributed further to the attrition of the Panzer IVs in Normandy and helped pin them in the British sector. In August for the renewed counter-attack at Mortain against the Americans the Germans could only gather seventy-seven Panzer Mark IVs and forty-seven Panthers, roughly the same inadequate number that had been launched in the initial attack, which involved fifty-seven Panzer IVs and seventy Panthers.

A few weeks later, unable to contain the American breakout, the German Army was in headlong flight and then trapped at Falaise and defeated. After the Battle for Normandy despite the presence of surviving panzers belonging to the SS at Arnhem, Montgomery was not put off launching Operation Market Garden that resulted in the disastrous battle for the Rhine crossing.

Following the Panzerwaffe's mauling in Normandy by late 1944 the Panzer IV was in very short supply. As a result of continual battlefield attrition and the disruption caused by Allied bombing the panzer divisions struggled to field both a battalion of Panzer IVs and a battalion of Panthers. The 2nd and 11th Panzer and the 2nd SS and 9th SS Panzer Divisions each had two companies of StuG assault guns instead of Panzer IVs; the 9th and 116th Panzer Divisions had no Panzer IV at all, fielding instead three companies of StuGs. Other divisions had a single battalion of mixed Panzer IVs and Panthers. The second battalion had to be substituted by panzerjäger and sturmgeschütz units.

To make up for such shortfalls, prior to Hitler's winter Ardennes offensive the 1st SS was supplemented by a battalion of heavy Tiger IIs, while the other divisions had to be brought up to some semblance of strength using StuGs and Jagdpanthers. The

1st SS ended up with a panzer regiment consisting of one battalion of mixed Panzer IVs and Panthers and one of Tigers. The division should also have had twenty-one Panzer IV/70 tank destroyers but its SS panzerjäger battalion only had ten on the eve of the battle. Nonetheless, a total of almost 140 Panzer IV/70 were available for the Ardennes offensive. The panzer divisions had Jagdpanzer IV and Panzer IV/70 tank destroyers equipping two companies of their panzerjäger battalion, the third company being equipped with towed anti-tank guns.

The 1st SS and 12th SS Panzer Divisions' Ardennes spearhead included 100 Panzer IVs. Two tank companies from 1st SS Panzer consisting of thirty-four Panzer IVs formed Kampfgruppe Peiper that led the daring attack toward Antwerp. The 1st SS also had a number of Flakpanzer IVs, which included Ostwind and Wirbelwind. Some of the latter were involved in the fighting at Stoumont where they acted in support of the infantry.

One knocked-out Panzer IV was photographed north-west of Bastogne. A massive explosion had shattered the glacis plate, tearing out the gearbox and differential assembly. The turret had also been blown off and rested on its side vertical to the hull. After the war this much-published image came to epitomize the Battle of the Bulge and the defeat of the panzers in North-west Europe.

Panzer IVs with the 12th SS Panzer Division on parade in France in early 1944. The majority of the Panzer IV deployed on occupation duties were Ausf H or J.

This 12th SS Ausf H has the side vision ports for the radio operator and the driver, indicating it is an early production version. It has the anti-aircraft machine gun fitted to the cupola and the one-piece hatch. It also has the latest drive sprocket but the mid-model idler. There is Zimmerit on the front of the turret.

The Schürzen on Ausf J '625' is in pristine condition and has been painted, along with the rest of the tank, in three-tone camouflage. The basic dunkel gelb has been oversprayed with irregular patches of oliv grun and rot brun. The tactical number was hand painted afterwards. The hull front and the gun mantlet have the zimmerit finish.

The crew of this tank in Normandy used track links to up-armour the glacis plate, the superstructure and even the front of the turret. It has the type three muzzle brake. What appear to be scorch marks around the driver and radio operator hatches suggests that it caught fire. It is possible the tank was deliberately torched by its crew after breaking down.

GIs examine a Hummel captured during the fighting in Normandy. It has a three-tone camouflage enhanced by foliage. It bears the national identification symbol and the tactical number '110'.

A StuG IV formerly serving with the 2nd SS Panzer Division captured during the Battle for Normandy. Although quicker to build, assault guns and tank destroyers were a distraction from Panzer IV gun tank production.

A sea of military debris. This Normandy scrapyard is full of discarded Panzer IVs. Around 750 saw combat in northern France.

This Ausf J was knocked out by Allied fighter-bombers in front of Patton's US 3rd Army during the Battle of the Bulge. Ironically the frame protruding from the cupola is the mount for an anti-aircraft machine gun.

This late-war Hummel was captured in April 1945 near Wurzen, Germany. An oliv grun pattern has been applied over the dunkel gelb, and the remains of foliage camouflage can be seen. The vehicle is undamaged and the gun is locked in the travelling position.

The victim of this concealed American M10 tank destroyer is a Panzer IV Ausf J.

Chapter Ten

Hitler's Rock

The Panzer IV proved to be the one constant in the Panzerwaffe's armoury during the Second World War. Like the T-34 it served throughout the conflict, although it was not built in sufficient numbers and up-gunned until late 1942 and early 1943, by which time it was too late. Hitler's hopes that he could step up production of the technically superior Panther and Tiger tanks never came to fruition because they were over-engineered and therefore difficult to mass-produce.

The Panzer IV appeared in ten different models (with three different guns) as well as a dozen different armoured fighting vehicles, whereas the T-34 essentially comprised two – the T-34/76 and T-34/85 (though to be fair there were five and three production models respectively of each, as well as half a dozen AFV variants). To put the Panzer IV's contribution in perspective, 8,500 were built compared with 55,000 T-34s. Nonetheless it proved to be one of the key if not best panzers of the Second World War and was Hitler's rock.

The Panzer IV proved to be quite a remarkable weapon. The Panzerwaffe recognized it for what it was – a robust and durable design. As a result it was the only German tank to remain in continuous production throughout the war, and was in production longer than any Allied tank. It was only rivalled by the Soviet T-34, which also stayed in production throughout. However, T-34 mass production did not commence until mid-1940, giving the Panzer IV a slight lead. In its favour the T-34 was almost impervious to the standard German 37mm and 50mm anti-tank guns, and of the Panzer III and IV, it outclassed the former in all respects and the latter in all except gun power where the up-gunned variants equalled it.

Due to the urgent need to find a counterpart to Soviet tank designs, production of the Panzer IV was in part marred by wasteful experimentation. This was because of Hitler's inability to standardize his tank force and settle on a single utilitarian design. He struggled with quality over quantity. As a result for example in October 1942 just 100 Mk IVs were built against about 900 T-34s.

From spring 1942 to the summer of 1943 just over 1,800 of the vastly improved Ausf F2 and G were built. It was not enough and many of them were swallowed up as combat replacements. In a similar timeframe, from spring 1943 to the summer of 1944, production was finally ramped up with almost 3,800 Ausf H, but after that production declined as the chassis was diverted to tank destroyers. The Panzer IV and indeed the Panther and Tiger could simply not compete with the enormous numbers of T-34s coming out of Stalin's factories.

Nonetheless, the Panzer IV accounted for over a third of German wartime tank production making it the most widely used tank of the war. It saw combat with the panzer divisions in all theatres of operation including Poland, France, the Balkans, North Africa, Russia, Italy and North-west Europe.

Manufacture of the Panzer IV easily outstripped that of the overrated Tiger and Panther combined. These totalled around 1,800 and 6,000 respectively. Panzer IV gun tank production amounted to over 8,500 – some 2,400 more than the Panzer III. When all the other variants using the Panzer IV chassis are taken into account, the overall total is 13,400. In contrast just over 6,100 Panzer III were built between 1937 and 1943. It proved far more useful as an assault gun platform with 8,600 StuG IIIs – the latter though were not tanks.

Hitler had to maintain Panzer IV production because of the German Army's constant urgent need for serviceable tanks. This prevented him from switching solely to the Panther and Tiger; however, this is certainly no reflection on the excellent basic design of the Panzer IV. Both the Panther and Tiger were labour intensive while they had exceedingly good anti-tank guns were often mechanically unreliable. Their weight strained the transmission and drive train and made them very difficult to recover. Once swamped by enemy tanks the Panther and Tiger's long-range stand-off kill capability was completely nullified.

Crucially the Panzer IV was much more reliable than both of them and at half their weight was easier to recover and repair. Like its key adversary, the T-34, the Panzer IV's design ensured that it could be regularly upgraded. American and British tanks did not offer such flexibility – the Sherman and Cromwell are prime examples of this very serious shortcoming.

Likewise, the size of the Panther and the Tiger proved a problem, making them easier targets. Panzer General von Manteuffel said the Panther 'would have been close to ideal' but for its high and bulky silhouette. The Tiger was almost 4m wide and 3m high, the Panther 3.5m wide and 3m high. The Panzer IV measured in at 2.8m and 2.7m (which included a bulkier cupola) respectively.

All these faults, it might be argued, permit the Panzer IV to steal the laurels as the best German tank of the Second World War. After the war such was its reputation that some surviving Panzer IVs even had a second career, seeing combat with the Syrian Army in the late 1960s. In contrast the Tiger and Panther never saw action again.

The early-model Panzer IVs were never intended as tank-to-tank weapons and suffered as a result. Once up-gunned the Panzer IV became the backbone of Hitler's panzer forces.

Late-model Panzer IVs being shipped to the front – in total over 8,500 Panzer IV were built along with almost 5,000 specialized AFV variants.

A Panzer IV lost during the fighting for Kharkov. The Panzer IV, along with the Panther and Tiger, proved a match for the T-34, but were never available in sufficient numbers in the face of growing attrition rates.

The snow-covered remains of an Ausf J, the very last model Panzer IV. Nearly 1,800 of these were built by the end of the war

Frozen Panzer IVs lost on the Eastern Front – some 6,100 Panzer IVs were lost to the Red Army.

The successful Panzer IV-based Hummel made its debut at Kursk and fought to the very end on the streets of Berlin. The gunners of this early model have been distracted from their target by something going on behind them

GIs souvenir-hunt amongst the wreckage of a Panzer IV.

One of the very last Hummels, destroyed during the battle for Berlin in April 1945.

An abandoned late-model Hummel self-propelled gun left in its firing position.

Further Reading

Tucker-Jones, Anthony, illustrated by Hemingway, David Lee, *Images of War Special: The Panther Tank, Hitler's T-34 Killer* (Pen & Sword Military, 2016)

Tucker-Jones, Anthony, *Images of War: German Assault Guns and Tank Destroyers 1940-1945* (Pen & Sword Military, 2016)

Tucker-Jones, Anthony, illustrated by Hemingway, David Lee, *Images of War Special: T-34. The Red Army's Legendary Medium Tank* (Pen & Sword Military, 2015)

Tucker-Jones, Anthony, illustrated by Delf, Brian, *Images of War Special: Tiger I & Tiger II* (Pen & Sword Military, 2013)